THEIR GOLDEN DREAMS

Willard Thompson

Copyright © 2015 Willard Thompson

This book is a work of fiction. All persons, places and events depicted herein, except those clearly in the public domain, are figments of the author's imagination or are used fictionally. Any resemblance to actual persons, living or dead, is unintentional

All rights reserved. No part of this book may be reproduced or transmitted in any form or by any means, electronic or mechanical, including photocopying, recoding or by any information storage and retrieval system—except by a reviewer who may quote brief passages in a review to be printed in a magazine, Newspaper or on the Internet—without written permission in writing from the publisher. For Information address Rincon Publishing, 1419 East Valley Road, Santa Barbara, CA 93108

Cover art: "San Francisco in 1850" Oil on canvas, by George Henry Burgess, 1878

Thompson, Willard, 1940-
Their golden dreams / Willard Thompson.
-- Santa Barbara, California : Rincon Publishing, [2015] pages ; cm.
(Chronicles of California)
ISBN: 13-digit: 978-0-9797552-7-9 ; 10-digit: 0-9797552-7-1
1. California--History--1846-1850--Fiction. 2. California--Gold discoveries--1846-1850--Fiction. 3. Gold mines and mining-- California--History--1846-1850--Fiction. 4. Sierra Nevada (Calif. and Nev.)--Social life and customs--19th century--Fiction. 5. San Francisco Bay Area (Calif.)--Social life and customs--19th century--Fiction. 6. Frontier and pioneer life--California--Fiction. 7. Gold miners--California-Fiction. 8. Women gold miners--California--Fiction. 9. Pioneers--California--Fiction. 10. Women pioneers--California-- Fiction. 11.Historical fiction.
I. Title. II. Series.
PS3620.H698 G65 2015
813./6--dc23 1505

Rincon Publishing

Santa Barbara, California

www.WillardThompsonBooks.com

THEIR GOLDEN DREAMS

Willard Thompson

SANTA BARBARA, CALIFORNIA

Christmas Day, 1846

DIEGO'S MOTHER DIDN'T move when the priest's Christmas blessing had faded away in the mission church. She sat rigid on the wooden bench. He sat beside her, looking up into her face, waiting for her signal to rise, but she continued to look straight ahead. The stone walls seemed to be pressing in on him. He felt as if the *araña de las candelas* hanging from the rafters might crash down at any moment so he started to rise. She pulled him down. He gave her a questioning look, then relaxed back on the bench.

She waited while the rest of the congregation rose and filed out, looking away from her as they passed. When the church was almost empty she reached for his hand. With his help, she slowly pulled herself up. The bulge under her long dress caused her to waddle toward the heavy wooden doors. He remembered how beautiful she had been before, but now she seemed ugly, misshapen and awkward and unhappy most of the time. He didn't understand the swelling. It had been unnoticed at first, but now he couldn't bear to look at her. He worried she might be sick, dying even, and he didn't know what to do.

Outside the mission, pewter and slate-colored clouds pressed the sky hard into the hilltop. As far as he could see out over the ocean to the islands, a solid mass of storm seemed poised to unleash its driving winds and torrential rain any minute.

She was moving more quickly now, leading him away from the

other worshipers toward the carriage where Victoriano waited to take them back to Cañada del Corral. The old Indian gripped the horses' reins with gnarled hands, restraining the impatient team of matched roan mares. Diego was anxious to hurry home, too, to find shelter from the coming downpour for Viento, his beloved horse.

With a hurried step that made the hem of his robe swirl about his feet, the priest came toward them. Diego darted a look at Victoriano, as if to plead with him to get the carriage moving. His mother quickened her steps too, but the priest intercepted them.

"*Buenos Dias*, Señora Austen." He inserted himself between her and the carriage, giving a weak, perfunctory smile. "*Feliz Navidad*. A joyous day, no? I bid you a blessed Christmas." He stopped talking to look around at the departing worshipers, a mix of rancheros with weather-creased faces and other men, fancy in frock coats, cravats and vests. The dark-haired women and young girls wore long, gay, multi-colored dresses with woolen shawls or embroidered silk mantons over their shoulders. Lace mantillas covered their heads.

"Your time comes soon and I understand that you came for the Sacrament. But I must tell you it is not proper for you to be in public," the priest said.

She bowed slightly and returned his vague smile. "Not proper, Padre?"

Diego dropped her hand and went to stand by the horses, away from the priest. He stroked one of the mares and watched the conversation, not understanding, but wishing they'd finish so Victoriano could drive them home.

"We have had this talk before, Señora, last spring when you fornicated with the New England man who has left you unmarried. Now your time comes. It is unseemly to appear at Mass."

She turned away to stare out over the town lying at the foot of

Mission Hill, and beyond, over the almost black, wind-whipped waters of the Santa Barbara Channel. She gave a deep sigh but didn't respond.

"Señora, see how the others avoid you. Surely, you see—"

She interrupted before he could finish. "On a day when we celebrate the birth of the Christ child? How could they shun me, Padre? How could you?"

The priest dropped his head. His sandaled foot drew a nervous pattern in the dust. When he looked up again it was only to acknowledge Don Nicholas Bell approaching.

"*Feliz Navidad*, Señora Austen, Padre Rubio. A joyous day, but not one to linger here too long, I think." Nicholas Bell was an American-born ranchero. Tall and lean, he was in his late forties but retained his youthful look and vigor. He doffed his sombrero to Delfina Austen, showing a full head of brown hair with only an occasional streak of gray.

Delfina gave Bell a smile in return. Rubio nodded to him.

"We should all take shelter, but I wanted a private word with Señora Austen."

"Do I intrude, then, Padre?"

"I was pointing out that the Señora's time approaches quickly and she should confine herself ..."

"He was embarrassed by the sight of me," Delfina interrupted.

"Really, Padre? Embarrassed? You should be glad to have a new member of your congregation arriving soon. To see the Señora in the bloom of motherhood seems a Christmas bright spot in the gloom brought on by this war."

The conversation puzzled Diego.

"Still, a woman in her condition is expected to confine herself until after the birth."

"Would you have preferred to ride in the rain all the way out to her rancho this afternoon to serve her the sacrament, Father?"

Rubio said nothing. He turned to look at the departing worshipers, then at the storm racing toward them from the south. "Pardon me," he said, starting to walk away. "I must greet the others."

Bell stared after him. He waited just a moment before turning back and calling out to Diego. "Are you helping your mother? You must do whatever she asks of you during these difficult times. How old are you now, son?"

"Eleven, Señor." Then Diego turned back to the horses thinking he always helped his mother. What was different now?

"Almost a man then, Diego. See that you respect your mother."

"We haven't seen you at the rancho for some time, Señor Bell." Delfina said. "*Como ésta tu niña?*"

"*Bien Señora, tiene diez años ahora.*"

"*Ésta bien.*" Delfina paused and looked directly at Bell, speaking English again. "Do you still want to buy the horses we broke for you this fall?"

Avoiding eye contact with her, he looked back at the priest disappearing into the mission. Scuffing his boots a little in the dirt, he shifted from his left to his right foot. After a moment, he gave her a pained look. "These are difficult times..."

"You do not want the horses then?"

"No, no, I don't mean that. I meant with the war... Señora, it is difficult to know what to do. Everyone is on his guard. I miss coming to your rancho, but... The war has changed us."

She took hold of the carriage side for support. The first hint of emotion showed in her voice. "Look at us. Now we say Señor Bell and Señora Austen. Once we were Don Nicholas and Doña Delfina ...and Will Thornton. The three of us. Always friends." She blotted a tear from her cheek. "The war has done this."

"I will come soon for the horses." Bell moved closer to her

and put his large hand on her shoulder. "I have missed you."

She flinched, so he removed his hand.

"I need the money. Other rancheros have asked for those horses so they can ride to the fighting..."

"Tell me how you are doing, Delfina. Is there something I can do for you? It isn't right that we should be on opposite sides after the years the three of us..." he hesitated. ... "The three of us were such fine friends."

"It *isn't* right. Californios and Yankees have always been friends."

"Things will be as they were before when the war ends."

"Ha! When the war ends it will no longer be my country. It will be yours. The time for us Californios is over, Señor Bell."

"Perhaps. But I promise, when the war ends we will treat your people as equals. We will all be better off under American rule."

She looked at him without replying.

He stood back. The smile faded from his face. "I hope that Will Thornton returns to you quickly when peace is settled. He loved you very much." Bell started to walk off but turned back again. "I will come to your rancho in the next several days to take the horses and pay you."

Two days of slashing rain built the torrent of water raging in the creek to the verge of overflowing its banks. Diego was like a prisoner inside the hacienda. He waited impatiently for any break in the unyielding storm so he could go into the corral with the wonderful Christmas gift his mother had given him. All he could do was marvel at the intricate craftsmanship of the hand-tooled silver bridle and braided rawhide reins, picturing how enviously the other young *caballeros* would admire them as he sat astride Viento.

The sun broke through on the third day. Storm clouds retreated over the high mountains behind the rancho, dissipating into silvery wisps that disappeared in a clear cerulean sky. Everything seemed clean, restored. Diego wasted no time running out to the corral where Victoriano and the other vaqueros were already mucking straw and manure from the muddy ground.

"*Hola*... hello, Diego," Victoriano greeted him, pointing at the bridle. "You will be ... proud *caballero*... when *Nuevo Año* begins."

Diego returned the old man's awkward grin. "Mama says we must use the American words when we can."

Holding his mother's gift, he went into the tack shed to get a brush before entering the corral. Twenty or more young mares and geldings stood patiently along the fence rails, steam rising from their wet hides as the sun warmed them. When he whistled, Viento returned a neigh and trotted across the corral to nuzzle his hand and stand patiently. With the stiff brush Diego removed all trace of mud from the mane and tail of the light-colored chestnut. He brushed Viento's hide to a sleekness that shone. When he was satisfied, he slipped the new bridle over his horse's head and offered the bit.

Victoriano came to stand beside him. He was an ageless man, a vaquero on the rancho since Josefa owned it and Delfina had been younger than Diego was now. A quiet man, he kept to himself, but guarded Delfina and Diego as if they were his own children. "You are a fine... young *hombre*," he said, smiling as he mixed the old language with the new. "When the... *niño* arrives your mother will need our help. You and I must take on more chores."

Diego stopped brushing Viento. He stood motionless for a moment. Then he looked into Victoriano's weathered face. "*Niño?*"

"*Oh, Sí, como no?* Yes... *un niño*...Baby."

The old man and the boy looked at each other for several

moments. A knowing smile spread over Victoriano's face, deepening the fleshy jowls that ran down from his cheeks to his chin, and showing places where teeth were missing. "Has your mother not told you?"

"Told me what?"

"About the baby. Soon, very soon, I think, you will have a brother or sister."

Diego was stunned. "A baby?" He thought for a moment. "My father has been dead more than four years."

"Not your father."

Diego gave Victoriano a puzzled look. "Señor Thornton?"

The old Indian nodded.

Diego moved away. He found an open place on the corral fence to lean against so he could think. He had never considered that he might have a brother or sister. He still carried resentment that his father's place had been taken by another man. Staring up the path at the hacienda, he thought about his mother and Will Thornton, and his thoughts turned to how much he missed his father. As he did, his breath caught in his throat. He blinked and looked again. A party of a dozen horsemen, clad in shabby buckskins, was riding down the path from the main trail. They were flanked by two soldiers carrying rifles and led by a man in an American military uniform.

Frozen momentarily, Diego ran back to the shed to grab a rifle off the rack. He came back out to confront the approaching party, thinking it was what his father would have done.

"*No, joven*," Victoriano shouted, coming across the ground to block him. "*Estos son hombres peligrosos.* Dangerous."

Fear struck Diego as he faced the soldiers, but someone had to protect his mother. He was scared, but his father had told him often a man had to do things he was afraid of doing. He planted his feet wide apart twenty yards from the riders, and brought the rifle to his shoulder.

The mounted men halted. The two men in front aimed their rifles at Diego.

"I shoot if you come near, enemy," he called out, uncertainty in his voice.

He could see the two soldiers fingering the triggers of their rifles. His throat felt thick. He kept his weapon tight against his shoulder, looking down the barrel at the officer in front. In that moment if he could have dropped the rifle and fled he would have, but for the thought of his mother, unprotected inside the house. His father's words rang in his ear. If only his father stood beside him.

"Put your rifle down, son," the officer called to him. "We are not here to fight."

"Put your rifles down then," he answered.

The officer made a motion to the two soldiers. "He's only a child."

Diego bristled. He stood taller. He gripped the rifle stock so tightly he felt a pain in his hand that ran up his arm.

From the back of the pack Nicholas Bell urged his horse forward to stop alongside the officer. "They will not hurt you, Diego," he shouted across the space between them. "We have come to see your mother. Lay your rifle down so they can see you won't shoot them. Then go fetch her, please."

Diego still wasn't convinced, but Bell's familiar voice calmed him some. It offered him a way out of the standoff. After another moment he knelt and set the rifle on the ground. Then he stood, his hands jammed on his hips, still confronting the riders.

"What is this? What are you doing, *M'hijo?*" Delfina came running from the casa. When she got to his side she grabbed him into her arms. Victoriano moved to stand beside her.

"Why have you come here, Señor Bell? Why have you brought all these *soldados* with you?"

Embarrassed, Diego struggled to free himself from his mother's arms and stand on his own, but he still held onto her hand and he could feel her hand shaking.

"Your horses, Señora Austen. As we spoke about after Mass."

"My horses? Why did you bring the American *soldados* with you?"

"I have brought Captain John Charles Frémont with me." Bell dismounted and came toward her.

The American officer took off his hat, but remained in the saddle.

"Captain Frémont arrived in Santa Barbara on Christmas eve, bringing his men with him over the mountains before the storm."

Frémont now dismounted and walked up to her. He made a sweeping bow so that the campaign hat he held in his hand brushed the ground. "Good day, Madam. You have trained your son well. He is a brave little soldier. But be careful for him in these difficult times that he does not get hurt."

Delfina didn't respond. She waited.

"For lack of good mounts many of my men had to walk to Santa Barbara carrying their saddles," Frémont told her. "The Californios along the way refused to sell me horses. Bell told me you bred the finest horseflesh in the region so I begged him to bring me to you." Again he offered a formal bow. "I need all that you can supply."

Diego felt his mother's fingers tighten on his hand. The color drained from her face. She looked from Frémont to Bell and back to Frémont.

"I am sorry, Captain. All the horses you see here were bred and broken for Señor Bell. I have no other horses."

Bell stepped forward. "I have agreed to relinquish these horses to the Army."

When Diego looked at his mother again there were tears in her eyes. The scared feeling grew in him.

"I cannot sell you my horses, Captain Frémont," Tears were running down her cheeks. She dropped Diego's hand to wipe them away. Then she straightened herself and addressed Frémont and Bell together. "I agreed to sell Don Nicholas my horses so he could work his cattle. Since then many of my neighbors have come to me for horses so they could ride off to fight Americans. I refused to sell them, saying they were promised—"

"Fortunate for you, you did. If you had sold them we could have arrested you for helping our enemies."

Delfina took several steps toward Frémont and stood directly in front of him. Standing straight now, her turquoise eyes flashed with anger. There were no longer any tears. "I will not sell you my horses. I will not allow you to use them against my people."

Frémont stepped back from her, startled by her aggressive stance and strident voice. He pulled himself erect. He had a new expression on his face.

"Madam, this conversation is wasting my time. You do not have the right to refuse me. I am taking your horses for the army of the United States and—"

"Arrest me if you must."

Bell moved close to Delfina. "Don't worry, *Señora*. I will pay the price for these fine mounts. Everyone will know you did not willingly sell to the American army."

"No, sir, you will not. I am requisitioning these horses for the army. My government will compensate the *Señora* for them. We do not steal them."

"But Captain Frémont, she needs the money now. To survive the winter. She depends on the sale of these horses."

"Round up all the horses in the corral," Frémont shouted

to his men. "Each of you take two or three." Turning back to Delfina, he took a sheet of paper from inside his hat. "Here is a voucher for all your horses. I believe I have been generous with you, Madam. When the war ends you will receive compensation from my government for your loss. Round them up!" he shouted again. "Get a move on, it'll be a slow ride back to town."

"No! You cannot do this." Diego ran up to Frémont. When he got there he was uncertain what to do but stood unmoving.

"Hush, boy. Don't get in the way of my men."

Delfina pulled Diego back from the captain. He could only watch as the Americans swarmed into the corral, gathering the horses and leading them out.

He broke away from his mother's grasp a second time. "No!" He raced toward a soldier who was holding Viento and two other horses by their lead ropes. "No!" he shouted again, "That is my horse! You cannot take him." He began hitting at the soldier with his fists, shouting "No. No!" over and over.

Victoriano tried to pull him away from the soldier.

"All the horses," Frémont shouted over him, and remounted his own horse.

The men moved quickly to remount, each with one or two of Delfina's horses securely tied to the pommels of their saddles. As they started off, Frémont stopped and jumped down from his mount. Moving quickly to where Viento waited with the other animals, he yanked the bit from the mare's mouth, jerked the bridle over her head and threw them on the ground.

Diego strained against Victoriano's firm grip.

"I am not a thief," Frémont shouted over his shoulder. "I take only the horses." He remounted and led the party back to the main trail.

CHAPTER 2

1850

THE EARLY MORNING sun reflected off the Santa Ynez Mountains, bathing Cañada del Corral in golden light. The corral hummed with activity. Diego was readying his horse for the long ride north when his mother called from the casa's veranda. It was not his beloved Viento, but one of the horses she had bred since Frémont's wartime raid four years ago.

"I said you are not to ride with the vaqueros," she called to him.

Diego paid her no attention. He continued adjusting the silver bit so it sat comfortably in his gelding's mouth. He tossed the braided reins over the horse's head and adjusted his stirrups. The four *vaqueros* in the corral with him were busy saddling their own horses, and securing a week's supply of food on the pack animals.

Hurrying into the corral, his mother stopped in front of him. "I told you no, *M'hijo*! Victoriano and the other men will take the herd north. You will stay with me."

"I am going with them."

"The trail is dangerous. Stay with me and your brother—"

"I'm riding with the herd, Mama, I am not afraid. I'm almost grown. You cannot stop me."

Victoriano moved from his horse to stand alongside Delfina.

"If you give your permission for him to ride with us, Señora Austen, we will look out for the boy. The drive might be good for him. I have watched his anger and restlessness grow the last few years."

"Since the war. What could I do?"

"Before that, Señora. Since his father's death. You protect him too much."

Delfina's face saddened. She nodded, but didn't speak.

"If he rides with us I will watch out for him. Perhaps the drive will help him grow up."

"I can take care of myself, Victoriano," Diego snapped. "I do not need you!"

Victoriano stepped closer to him. "You are still a pup. Some at fourteen are men. But you are not yet a man. If Señor Austen were alive... Your mother has done her best."

"Please stay with me," Delfina said.

"You treat me like a child, Mama. This is a chance for me."

"Timeteo can stay behind to protect you," Victoriano assured her.

Delfina looked from her son to the white-whiskered Indian. "You may have more wisdom than I do, Victoriano. The drive might be good for him. I hope so. Bring him back safely, and get a good price for the cattle. We need the gold."

Victoriano looked at the ground. "The trail back will be dangerous. Returning rancheros speak of *banditos*, but we will watch out for Diego."

"I am not afraid of bandits," Diego boasted. "I have my rifle and pistol. No one can scare me."

Delfina and Victoriano exchanged looks.

Stockton pulsed with activity. Diego had never seen a town like it. "*Así que muchas personas!*" he said in Spanish, the language vaqueros used on the cattle drive, He reined his horse alongside Victoriano's, and leaning forward in the saddle. "*Nunca he visto tantos hombres. Nunca en Santa Bárbara.*"

The old vaquero chided him. "Speak English now, Diego. It's because of the gold. Here the miners buy supplies for the diggings in the hills, or spend their gold on other things. Here we sell the cattle. Then we go back."

Everywhere Diego looked canvas tents, competing with each other for miners' gold, filled the landscape. Some tents offered shovels, pans and boots, all displayed on the ground in front. Others held clothing, utensils and bedding stacked tent-high inside. Still other tents rented sleeping shelters for the throng of men that milled around the village. On the river, an armada of boats of various sizes and sail patterns, and a few small steamers, vied for places to unload fresh cargo alongside the barrels and crates already stacked along the banks.

"Will we camp here tonight, Victoriano? I want to see the village."

"Yes, we camp, but you will stay with me until we start back to the rancho. We go now to see the cattle buyers."

When the cattle sale was completed, his hand resting on the butt of his pistol and his eyes scanning for trouble, Victoriano packed the leather pouches of gold deep into his saddlebags and they rode back to the camp. "Rest tonight, tomorrow we ride south again," he told Diego and the other vaqueros.

Diego lay around the camp that afternoon. As evening came on the other vaqueros drifted into the tent city looking for something to do. Victoriano stayed to himself, resting, using his saddle for a pillow, his pistol and rifle always ready on the blanket beside him. As dusk settled in, deepening the shadows of the tall bay trees and willows, the fatigue of the long drive finally overtook the old Indian. He slumped lower against his saddle. His head nodded off to one side. His eyelids fluttered and then closed. Diego watched until he was sure Victoriano was asleep, then he quietly left the camp and walked into town.

He merged into the stream of men flowing back and forth between the tents along the river like a restless sea. Many were Yankees, about the same number spoke Spanish with unfamiliar accents. He inspected the mining tools and clothing displayed in several tents he passed, but they held no interest for him. Aimlessly, he followed a group entering a large tent to see what was drawing them in. As the tide of men pushed him toward the back of the tent, he thought about turning back, but the pressure was too great.

"Whisky, Mate?"

"Huh?"

"I said ya here for a shot of whisky, ain't ya? Speak up, Mate." A bearded man standing behind a makeshift wooden bar glared at him. "There's plenty behind ya with a thirst. Quarter ounce of gold will wet yer whistle."

Looking around, Diego saw that the crowd of miners was pressed against the bar on both sides of him. Behind the bar, men moved up and down pouring shots from bottles for the men who tossed small nuggets to them.

"No, no whisky. I don't have gold."

"You must be the only poor son of a whore without a few grains of dust for a snort in Stockton, Mate. Best you move on then."

Diego shrugged and turned away as several other men fought to take his place.

"*Une minute*," the man beside him called out. "I pay. Whisky *pour mon pauvre nouvel ami*."

The barkeeper shrugged indifference. He set a tumbler on the bar and took a small nugget from the man. Then he poured from the bottle.

Diego looked at the stranger, a tall young man, thick hair hanging over his forehead, and a dark complexion. The man smiled. "Drink up, *mon ami*."

When he raised the glass to his lips and sipped, the whisky burned in his throat and continued down into his stomach. He winced. The man beside him grinned. "Best to toss it all down at once. It's terrible swill, you know, nothing like the fine wines we have at home. But it gets the job done."

Diego swallowed the remainder of the shot. The burn grew so strong he though he would gag. His eyes began to water. Then, embarrassed, he straightened up and looked at the man. "*Gracias*. Thank you. I've never had whisky before."

"Takes some getting used to, doesn't it? You new here? Come along outside where it's quiet. We can talk. My name is Luc Benard."

Diego followed Benard, wondering why the young man, at least ten years older than he was, with the strange accent, was being nice to him. Not an American, that was certain.

"What was the language you were speaking?" he asked Benard as they went.

They found a vacant spot outside along the riverbank and sat on the ground leaning back against a bay tree. "I'm from France. Had to learn enough English to come to California. I was new here not long ago, like you. Got here early in '49. You looked frightened in there. I hope I am not being too bold. What is your name?"

Diego introduced himself to Luc Benard. He didn't know where France was, but didn't ask. They settled into an easy conversation. He told Benard about driving cattle from Santa Barbara to Stockton. Benard told him about the fighting in the streets of Paris. He said he had joined a group of men to come to the gold fields.

Diego listened intently. "What's it like up there?" He asked.

"Beautiful country. Hard work, of course. Streams are cold, but we're using a long tom and sharing the work and the gold. Plenty of it so far if you work for it. Californio, aren't you?"

"Mother's a Californio, my father was from New York. Dead now. Stallion kicked him in the head when I was younger."

"Too bad. You seem like a nice fellow, Diego. Would you like to join us? I'm camped yonder on the way north. We could ride up to Angels Camp together. You could share in the work. Might be safer for a young man like you."

"Don't know. Like to. It sounds exciting, but I should go back to my mother's rancho with the vaqueros. I'd like to see more of the land up here though. Nothing much in Santa Barbara. Not like here."

They talked a while longer. Then Diego thanked Benard and made his way in the darkness back to camp on the outskirts of the village. As he walked along the path on the far side of the river, he thought about his conversation with Benard. There was plenty of gold in the rivers if you worked for it, Benard had said. His mother needed gold, maybe she needed more than Victoriano was taking back to her. The thought played in his head as he walked on.

Back in camp, he lay down as far from Victoriano as he could get. He couldn't sleep. All night long he tossed on his blanket thinking about what Luc Benard had said about the gold diggings, and thinking about helping his mother. Toward morning, after the moon had set, but while the bright northern star still shimmered overhead, Diego picked up his blanket and crept off to his horse. Behind him he thought he heard Victoriano or one of the other vaqueros stirring. He didn't look back, and, as the sky began to brighten, he found the Frenchman's camp.

In Boston, Massachusetts, eighteen-year-old Hannah Runyon took a deep breath, squared her shoulders and knocked on the door of the morning room in the Back Bay townhouse where she'd grown up. A four-story building, just a bit smaller than others on the block so that it could be wedged in between two older brownstones, it had been built by Captain Benjamin Gray in the 1830s, when he married Hannah's mother and accepted Hannah as part of the bargain.

She waited to be invited in, then, clutching the letter in her left hand, she slowly turned the brass handle. Faint, familiar smells of wood polish and verbena perfume greeted her. Six carved, upholstered rosewood chairs near the entrance surrounded a rectangular ebony table with brass fittings. She stopped behind the table, setting the letter down and smoothed her long skirt over her petticoats. At the far end of the room, her mother, Brigid Gray, sat at a small drop leaf writing desk. The room was decorated with paintings and artifacts Captain Gray had collected on his trading voyages around the world. A large window looked down on people hurrying along the street below, the men holding their bowlers tight to their heads and the women protecting their long skirts and petticoats against the force of the brisk breeze. The only sound in the room came from a walnut grandfather clock in a far corner ticking off the seconds until Hannah would face the deluge.

Looking up from the desk, her mother smiled a greeting. "What brings you here so early, dear?"

Hannah paused for just an instant, gathering in a breath, then charged ahead. "A letter. A sailor delivered it just now. All the way from California, Mother. Imagine that, all the way from San Francisco. It's from Mister Parker."

"And who is Mister Parker?"

So it begins, Hannah thought, always putting me on the defensive. She controlled her flash of anger, but braced herself for what was to come. "You know who, Mother. Josiah Parker. He courted me last year."

Brigid's smile faded, replaced by what Hannah called her mother cat look.

"That Mister Parker, is it? He hasn't been around for a while. I thought you had stopped seeing him. Come sit over here dear. Tell me about the letter."

Hannah stayed standing by the table near the doorway, studying her mother's face for any hint of her mood, wondering what she might say next. "No Mother, we hadn't stopped courting." She took in a second breath. "Mister Parker went to California, I told you that. He writes me that he is doing well in the gold diggings." Summoning all her resolve, she added, "He has asked me to come to California to be his wife. He wants to marry me, Mother." She stopped and waited.

For a moment Brigid didn't respond. Hannah watched as she touched her hand to her auburn hair, its color dimmed with age. Then she put her hand to her mouth, breathing several times into her fist, as if trying to warm it. "Be his wife, yer sayin'?"

Hannah returned her mother's stare with an expressionless face, inwardly chuckling at how Brigid's Irishness always showed when she got excited.

"What a fine proposition from a lad with no trade to support a wife. And you just a lass of eighteen, with barely a clue about life. Well, it is simple enough, dear: Do not toy with him. Write him today and tell him—"

"Don't be so cruel, Mother. I want to marry him. We love each other." Hannah wondered at the bold words coming from her own mouth.

"Run off to California and marry him? Pray God, how will he support ya? I don't see what love's got to do with that."

"He writes that he is doing well. He says there is enough gold for him to bring me to California. He plans to start a small carpenter shop."

"How could that be, Hannah, when he couldn't find a trade here?"

"You're not being fair. He couldn't find a journeyman's position after he finished his apprenticeship. Woodworking is becoming a mill job. Things are changing in New England. You know that, I've heard you and the Captain speak of it. Mister Parker doesn't want to work in a mill, he's a craftsman."

"What kind of life will he be offering ya, do ya think?"

"A life we'll share. It will be our adventure together."

"Not likely, girl. More likely a life of scrubbing and cleaning and wiping babies' bottoms, always scrounging for food to keep 'em from screaming their heads off. That's the life you'll be choosin', I'm thinkin'. Not much of an adventure. I say no, Hannah. Break it off now. You can make a good marriage right here in Boston. You shan't go to California."

"I will go, Mother." Hannah startled both of them with the defiance in her voice.

"Hannah, listen to me. Life is harder than just being in love. I know."

"Don't tell me about my father again," Hannah burst out. "Will Thornton left you on the dock pregnant with me when he sailed off, I know that story."

"Watch your tongue! You'll be hearing it as long as I've breath to say it if it saves you from the life I've had. Time you listened. Men are idle dreamers."

"Mister Parker's different. He won't abandon me like my father abandoned you. We'll work together to build a life in California."

"Sure as I'm sitting here you'll be alone in a year." Brigid rose from her chair, rearranging her long dress so that it floated just above the carpet. "You'll come dragging back—probably clutching a babe—and beg us to take you in. You need to do some serious thinking about this before ya go running off, dear. I don't want you hurt the way Will Thornton hurt me."

Hannah stood in the doorway, staring at her mother. Tears formed in her eyes and she wiped them away. Anger welled in her breast. She stayed that way several moments, hearing her mother's words, as if they were needles pricking on her skin. The pendulum of the clock marked the passing of time. She smelled the verbena and struggled to maintain her courage.

"You're still bitter about being left alone with me. I'm sorry for that, Mother, but I won't let my life be like yours. I won't let it slip away in bitterness or nagging thoughts about what might have been. I'm going to California. Don't stop me."

CHAPTER 3

1851

HANNAH DEPARTED FROM Boston for California in the fall of 1850 under gray skies. By the time she boarded the steamer that would take her to New York, where her voyage to Panama and San Francisco would really begin, all the harsh words and angry rebuttals between mother and daughter had been exhausted. At the dock Brigid complimented her daughter on her choice of traveling attire—a well-tailored, dark-colored dress with matching mantle. Hannah smiled and brushed a kiss lightly on her mother's cheek. Brigid returned the gesture, then waved a quick goodbye and left the dock.

A day later an ashen sky threatening snow hung over lower Manhattan. A chilling wind fretted the waters of the East River, bringing strong and unpleasant smells of New York's harbor to Hannah's nose as she boarded the steamship *Empire City* bound for Chargas, on the eastern side of the Isthmus of Panama. She didn't linger at the rail, hurrying instead down to the main deck where her cabin, containing four bunks, was near the aft salon. Three other women: two spinster sisters traveling together to New Orleans and an austere, plain-faced girl about Hannah's age, who introduced herself as Caroline Peabody, soon joined her.

"I'm being sent to Honolulu to teach school by the Board of Foreign Missions in Boston," Caroline told her cabin mates. I'm happy to be traveling with such fine Christian women."

Caroline was a wisp of a girl with straw-colored hair parted in the middle of her head and pulled back into a tight bun and covered with a muslin cap. She wore plain woolen dresses each day on the voyage south. She and Hannah had little in common beyond their age, but the paucity of young women on the *Empire City*, and the boredom of the journey, thrust them together, and they spent days in the gold and damask upholstered rosewood chairs in the ladies salon.

"I am thankful to have been called to do God's work among the savages," Caroline said. Around them the few other women traveling on the *Empire City* talked together in hushed voices.

"Aren't you just a little scared?"

"I am. I pray every night for the strength to conquer my fears."

"I'm scared of what lies ahead too."

"But you're going to meet your intended. There must be much joy in your heart."

"I hardly know Mister Parker really. I hope I'm not making a mistake."

"Oh... I see."

"I hope there's a future for me in California."

"But your mother? Your father?"

"I've been alone most of my life." Hannah stopped to consider her reply, and in that moment she heard a pinched-face, middle-aged woman seated across the salon raise her voice. The woman had an ample figure and brown sausage curls hanging down both sides of her face, hiding her ears. "... We're only going to be in California long enough to collect the gold," the woman was saying. "No more than a week or two I hope. A month at the most. Then we'll return to New Orleans. Mister Stillman promises to build me a large mansion out by the lake on our return."

"My father left before I was born," Hannah told Caroline. "My mother is very bitter about that. We don't spend much time together, but I carry her last name, not my father's. I've learned to get on by myself."

When the *Empire City* reached Chargas, the passengers were unloaded onto the beach alongside their baggage. It was a dismal village, surrounded by a muddy swamp, alive with insects and crawling with snakes and alligators. Wooden hovels dotted the edge of a dense jungle. Garbage floated in the Chargas River. The jungle hovered over it, blocking out sunlight, but trapping the stifling heat and stench.

Half naked men jabbered at the passengers in strange singsong voices, offering to paddle them in canoes up river to Las Cruces, the first stop on the overland journey across the isthmus.

"I am not meant for this kind of heat or these dark-skinned men," Hannah complained to Caroline as the natives pushed in close around them.

A frightened look came over Caroline's face. "They're savages. We might never be seen again if we got in a canoe with them."

"I hope it's cooler up river. Perhaps we should start soon."

Hannah shuddered at the mob of men milling around her. As she and Caroline tried to decide what they should do, Missus Stillman, the woman she'd overheard in the ladies' salon, pushed through the throng of natives toward them.

"Come along girls, it's all arranged," she called out. "Mister Stillman's worried about you. He's arranged for you to come with us on the little steamer to Las Cruces. You wouldn't be safe with these ruffians, he says, so he's paid your way. We'll travel together. You can call me Prudence. Point out your trunks so they can be loaded and hurry so we can leave this wretched place as soon as possible."

Their Golden Dreams

For days after the steamer left them in Las Cruces, Hannah, Caroline and the Stillmans, led by two hired guides, rode mules along jungle trails up and over the crest of the mountains, and then descended toward the Pacific coast. Hannah suffered the discomfort of the ride stoically. The dense jungle they passed through on the narrow trail enchanted her with its exotic foliage, but at the same time its vast, unending sameness horrified her. Trees were ominous giants towering over them. Shrill, wildly plumed birds protested their presence. Unseen creatures rustled through the undergrowth, seeming to run ahead as if conspiring to attack at some distant point. It was the monkeys that terrified Hannah most, swinging through the trees above, gibbering as they followed the travelers, and occasionally reaching down to touch her hair. She was in constant fear that this remote world would be the end of her brief life, with no accomplishments of note to show for it.

Cresting the final ridge, they looked down on Panama City, precariously perched on the shore of the Pacific Ocean. Its whitewashed buildings seemed to have been dropped randomly along narrow streets, like pebbles from the hand of a careless giant.

"Almost there," Hannah said brightly to Prudence Stillman and her husband, with an audible sigh of relief.

The party dismounted. Standing on the edge, looking down, they could hear faint church bells, chiming from spired steeples. The guides, impatient to reach the final destination, tried to urge them on, but the group stood in awe of the view.

"Thanks to you two we have made the crossing safely. I don't know how Caroline and I would have managed on our own." Hannah turned to Caroline, seeking agreement, but was startled when her companion turned away and dashed into the bushes holding her hands to her mouth. Hannah thought to follow but Prudence held out a restraining arm.

When Caroline reappeared minutes later, wiping her mouth with a lace handkerchief, Hannah cried out, "What's happened to you? You look terrible."

Caroline's face was flushed. Sweat beaded on her forehead. She was shaking so hard Hannah reached out to steady her. The skin of her arm felt like parchment to Hannah's touch. When she let go Caroline's skin kept the impression left by her fingers for several seconds. Caroline wobbled from side to side.

"Sorry," she said. "Could not help myself. It came over me all of a sudden."

Prudence Stillman looked worried. "We should get her to a doctor as quickly as possible."

Cholera was rampant in Panama City. The hospital was full of gaunt victims moaning their misery. Prudence Stillman recoiled from the sight of so many living skeletons. Some lay on soiled beds, but most were on straw mats or the hospital's bare dirt floor, a few already having passed on into the beyond. A harried doctor confirmed Caroline's cholera as he hurried by.

"We cannot stay here, Mister Stillman." A look of panic was in Prudence Stillman's eyes. She took his arm and pulled him away. "If we stay we may never get to San Francisco, never get our share of the gold. Come along. Mister Stillman! We've done our Christian duty. You come too, Hannah. We've done all we can for the girl. We must save ourselves now." Pulling her husband along, Prudence Stillman fled out the hospital door. Hannah watched them go. For an instant she considered going with them, then she turned back to Caroline.

Caroline's vomiting and diarrhea worsened. Her muscles began to cramp. She had almost no urine. With each hour her dehydration grew worse. Hannah took up a permanent station at her bedside, allowing only an American doctor, who was awaiting a steamship to San Francisco, to approach her. He shook his head and told Hannah only time would tell if Caroline would fight off the infection. Gripped by fear, Hannah thought about the Stillmans again, already seeking final passage to California while she tended this young woman she hadn't even known a month ago. She wanted to follow them out of the hospital. The thought nagged at her that others had always abandoned her. She promised herself she would keep Caroline Peabody alive and stay with her as long as it took. She began to wonder if she would ever see California or Mister Parker.

"What can I do?" She pleaded with the doctor.

"Fluids. Fluids and rest. Fluids, but not the water that comes from taps and fountains in the city. That's where the cholera comes from. She needs fluids." he said it again then shrugged. "Time will tell."

"You will not die," Hannah promised Caroline. "I couldn't bear to have you leave me." Hannah trembled with fear as she said it.

"God bless you," Caroline mumbled hoarsely.

She grew worse. Silently Hannah begged God to show his mercy. She held onto Caroline's hand, testing the resiliency of her skin from hour to hour. She bathed her in cool water several times a day and pressed damp towels to her forehead. When Caroline vomited or had a bout of diarrhea, she cleaned her up, trying to smile and reassure her as she did. She ventured into the town to find juices safe for her to drink and begged boiled water from the hospital staff. Caroline's death was unacceptable, as if it were an omen about her own life that lay ahead. She vowed to fight it with all her strength.

After ten days of her night and day vigil, when nothing seemed to have changed, Hannah, exhausted, was on the brink of losing hope. The next morning when she pinched Caroline's arm to test her dehydration her skin bounced back. In another day she was recovering but weak. It was a miracle of sorts, Hannah decided. Then she wondered had God used Caroline to test her? Or was this just the first of many tests ahead?

Peering from the deck of the Pacific Mail steamship *Tennessee*, Hannah could see San Francisco was not the city she had dreamed of or hoped for. Through the wispy fog that covered the hills like a veil, it seemed hardly a city at all. The bay behind her was crowded with abandoned ships swinging on their anchors, sending a ghost-like, unworldly sound over the water as a faint breeze hummed in their rigging. Barely seen wood and canvas tents on the flat land were a hodge-podge of sizes and shapes. Wooden buildings lined the shore, with even a beached sailing vessel pulled up between them. She could see nothing pleasant about San Francisco.

Caroline Peabody stood beside her, almost fully recovered on the voyage from Panama City, but still a little unsteady. When the ship docked, Hannah guided her down the gangplank. Caroline hailed a wagon as soon as a crewman delivered her trunk on the dock. She asked the driver to take her to the Commissioners of Foreign Missions' office and gave him a sheet of paper with the address printed on it. Then she quickly embraced Hannah and followed the driver across the muddy street and onto a wooden sidewalk, carrying her carpet bag while he pushed her small trunk on his handcart.

Even though surrounded by a crowd of men hurrying in all directions, Hannah felt abandoned—more alone than she had ever felt before—by the suddenness of Caroline's departure. Gone, just like that, hardly a farewell. Hannah was alone and scared.

"Can I be assisting you, lass? You be lookin' a bit muddled to me."

She heard the familiar Irish lilt. It brought a smile, bringing back her mother's voice as she was growing up. Her tension eased some. "Muddled I am," she laughed.

The young man standing at her side was of medium build with fair hair and blue eyes that reminded her of the transparent Caribbean waters she crossed on the way to Panama.

"M'name's Pádraig.

"Patrick?"

"Pádraig Duggan, I am. I'd be pleased to guide you wherever you want to go. And bring your trunk along with us into the bargain. Where are you heading?"

"That's just it. I'm going to Angels Camp, but I have no idea where that is or how I am supposed to get there."

"Angels Camp, is it? A far journey, I'd say. In the southern mines it is. You can't get there today, lass. A long day or two's travel, it be at best. Do you have a hotel in mind for the night? City Hotel up to the Plaza would be a safe place for a young miss like yourself. Tomorrow I can take you to a steamer bound for Stockton. From there you'll be close to Angels Camp."

Hannah let out a sigh. "You're a godsend. That would be fine. I'm fatigued. A night's rest on dry land would do me good."

"I'll guide you. I meet most all the steamers and help the passengers as much as I can."

Just before eight the next morning Pádraig Duggan was waiting in a heavy mist outside the hotel. Loading her trunk on his pushcart again, he led Hannah to the Vallejo Street wharf where a small, two-stacked, side-wheel steamer belched black smoke and tugged against its mooring lines. She gave him a couple of coins from her dwindling supply and thanked him.

"No gold, Miss?" he asked.

She smiled at him and shrugged. "Sorry."

Pádraig wiped the drops of moisture from his forehead and grimaced. "Not much use here for these," he said, handing them back. "You'll need gold when you come back to the City. You can pay me then."

She thanked him for his kindness and boarded.

As the steamer made its way across the bay toward Alcatraz Island, Hannah stood in the lee of the wheelhouse, which provided scant protection from the wind and mist. The dismal weather added to her feeling of desperation. It felt as if her whole world had slipped out of control. Alone, without friends, with no real idea what married life might be like, it was only her determination to prove her mother wrong that kept her going. And thinking about what Josiah Parker would be like only added to her mood. As the small ship turned to the north, passing the Golden Gate, she saw her old life floating away behind her in the ship's wake. The same feeling of intense loneliness that had gripped her when Caroline Peabody walked off was becoming a familiar companion. She trembled a little and clutched the rail tightly.

"Beggin' yer pardon, Miss, is everything all right? I couldn't help noticing you were crying."

She came back from her thoughts and looked at the tall, broad-shouldered man standing at her side, smiling down at her. She returned his smile and reached up a gloved hand to dab at her cheeks.

"I'm all right."

"You look scared to me."

"I guess I am. A little." She tried to hide a sniffle. "I only arrived in California yesterday and now I don't really know where I'm going. How long will it take us to get to Stockton?"

"Should be there by first light tomorrow."

Hannah looked around the deck at her fellow passengers.

"Am I the only woman on board?"

"Not many women going to Stockton. Don't you worry, Miss, there are a couple of women down below. No harm'll come to you if that's what you're thinking. How old you be?"

"Eighteen."

"My name's Brannan, Sam Brannan. Be my pleasure to escort a handsome young lady like yourself to Stockton."

"I'm not going to Stockton, I'm going to Angels Camp."

"So you're going up to the digging then?" Brannan rubbed his chin whiskers as he studied her. "What's taking you there?"

Hannah blushed. "I'm going to be married."

"Must be a lucky man waiting for you, all right. Aren't many fair young American women in the diggings, with sweet brown eyes and fair hair the color of Maine molasses like yours. Mostly just your dark-eyed Chilean *señoritas* at the fandangos in Angels Camp."

"How do I get there?"

"Stage coach is best—you won't want to ride horses or mules that far. Can't miss the stage. It's on the road by the landing."

"Are you going to the diggings too?"

"No, Miss. I'm not made for that kind of labor. More than one way to get gold besides catching your death of fever freezing in an icy river."

"Then what is it you do for gold?"

"I'm a merchant. All the forty-niners need picks, pans and shovels, Miss. I sell them. Just delivering a new supply to my store in Stockton is all. Then I'll head back down river. San Francisco's the best place for me."

Just after first light, with sun breaking through scattering clouds, the steamer rounded the last of the river's serpentine bends. Stockton lay dead ahead, another tent city like San Francisco, but on a smaller, shabbier scale. After a few minutes the ship nudged into a wooden dock along a levee where several smaller sailing vessels were tied up. The riverbank beyond the dock was a clutter of wooden boxes and barrels scattered around, some broken open, with all manner of supplies—tools, clothing, even flour and dried beans—spilling out. Across the river from the dock men hustled up and down a plank walkway. A row of canvas tents was alive with activity. It was all confusion to Hannah, an assault on her sense of orderliness. She shivered involuntarily, searching the shore for the stagecoach the man had promised, impatient to join Josiah Parker and yet still apprehensive.

A few yards off from the dock an empty stagecoach stood on the road at the end of the levee, as Sam Brannan had promised. Four impatient brown horses rattled their harness chains as they waited. Hannah hurried up to the rough-looking old man who stood alongside the coach. He was clad in buckskins, with a slouch hat on his head and muddy boots on his feet.

"Will you take me to Angels Camp?"

The driver looked her up and down. Then he scuffed the dirt in front of him with the toe of his boot and stared at the dust it kicked up.

Hannah waited. "Well," she said finally, "Will you take me or not?"

"It'll be crowded for a proper lady like yourself, Miss. Might be better if you waited 'til tomorrow."

"Crowded? I see no one in your stage. I can't wait until tomorrow."

"I've got three other women coming along in a few minutes. French women. Might not be pleasant."

Hannah gave the driver a look of rebuke. "I've no problem riding with strangers, sir, American, French or otherwise. Man or woman, it makes no difference to me. I must get to Angels Camp."

The driver shrugged. "If you don't mind riding with the French women climb aboard then. I'll fetch your trunk for ya, Miss, but don't say I didn't warn ya. We'll be off when they get here."

Hannah shrugged off the man's strange behavior and climbed into the coach. In a few minutes three young women, laughing together and talking loudly in French arrived. They were all similarly dressed in short cotton dresses, trimmed in lace at the bodice and hemline, that showed their white pantalets and ankle-high shoes. They pointed at her, and giggled among themselves before boarding the stagecoach. One sat on the bench beside her and the other two sat facing her. Still giggling, in halting English they introduced themselves as Clarisse, Adrienne and Miette, but Hannah was not sure which girl went with which name. Two of them were clearly on the cusp between their twenties and thirties, with dark hair, well powdered faces and bright red lips. The one she thought was Miette was younger. Her coal black hair was a tangle of curls that hung down to just above her shoulders. Her eyes were amber in color, glistening against the contrast of heavy lashes and dark brows. Hannah thought her by far the prettiest of the trio.

They began peppering her with questions. "Why are you going to Angels Camp, *mademoiselle*?" one asked, her lips turned up in a smile that showed a dimple in her right cheek.

For the second time Hannah explained her journey.

"Ah, to marry your beau. *Tres bien*."

"And you? Why do you go to Angels Camp?" Hannah responded.

"*Bien sûr, mademoiselle, nous sommes actrices.* Entertainers." The women looked to each other, nodding agreement.

"Entertainers. What will you do in Angels Camp?"

The trio traded smiles among themselves. "*Oui*. We sing and dance. We entertain the men in the *champs aurifères* who crave our company after their hard day's work."

After the initial flurry of conversation, the French girls spent most of the daylong stagecoach ride into the foothills talking among themselves. Hannah was pleased to be left alone with her musings about Josiah Parker and what she might find when they arrived in Angels Camp. She took one of the stagecoach's heavy wool robes and pulled it tight around her, dozed off and on as the stage bounced and rolled from side to side following a trail across the flat lands around Stockton. She could feel the horses beginning to strain against their braces on the uphill grade. At times she admired the scene as the trail wound through pine and fir forests with rolling green hills in the distance. Other times, closing her eyes, she tried to envision her reunion with Josiah Parker.

It was late afternoon when the driver finally reined the horses to a halt. Hannah came fully awake and stared out the stagecoach windows. The horses had stopped in front of a large structure held together with rough nails. Similar buildings lined the main, hard-packed dirt street. Hannah gasped at the shoddiness of the tiny village of Angels Camp.

"We are here, *filles*," whispered one of the girls. "Look *de toute beauté*, beautiful," the one she thought was Miette said. She smiled, showing the dimple in her cheek, and immediately began primping the ringlets of her hair.

A crowd of twenty or thirty overall-clad men, their woolen shirts showing signs of heavy wear, began gathering around the coach, shouting to one another about the arrival of the "French girls". When the coach door opened they let out a roar of greeting. Hannah held back, waiting for the trio, led by Miette, who pushed her two companions out of the way in order to be first, stepped down. She gave the miners a toothsome smile and a flutter of her lashes, and waved a delicately gloved hand. The other two, each trying to outdo the other in coquettishness, followed. Led by Miette they lifted their skirts just a little and did an impromptu dance on the plank sidewalk in front of the building that boasted a large, hand painted sign proclaiming the Angels Camp Saloon and Gaming Hall. The men gathered around them roared approval. More men came pouring out of the building to join those already cheering.

"They're here," the men shouted almost in unison. "The girls are here. Let's celebrate, boys! Look at that one." Someone pointed to Hannah, the last woman to step down from the stagecoach. "Fair skin, dark brown hair. What a beauty. Come on, boys, back to the bar. Let's buy 'em a drink."

The crush of the men jamming into the saloon pushed Hannah and the French girls forward like an irrepressible wave. She tried to resist, but the force was too strong. Instantly surrounded, she protested, "No! No! I'm not one of them," but the miners paid her no heed. Several hands pressed on her back, forcing her deeper into the large room. Her fear rose.

"What's your drink, darlin'?" A portly chap, reeking of sweat and whisky, and old enough to be her father, took her by the arm. He smiled at her, revealing a gap where a tooth should have been. "Let me get it for ya."

She pulled her arm away, and struggled to resist the crowd pushing her forward, as she frantically searched the sea of faces for Mister Parker. Her fear rose to a level where faintness came over her when she realized he was not among the miners. Dear God, she thought, what will they do to me? Her panic took over.

A dark complexioned man saw her distress and rushed to her side as she started to melt onto the floor. He pushed the other miner away and caught her in his arms, shouting to the other men to clear a path. He took her out the door where she was able to take several deep breaths.

"I'm not with the other girls," Hannah said weakly, trying to regain her composure. "I came to meet Josiah Parker. Do you know him? I didn't see him in the crowd."

The man looked around. "Maybe that's him coming down the road. You'll be okay now."

"I didn't know you were on the stage," Josiah Parker said breathlessly as he rushed up to them. "Lucky I was at the store when it arrived. Saw you and came as fast as I could."

"Mister Parker... I was so afraid ...I... I don't know what might have happened if this gentleman hadn't rescued me."

Josiah Parker extended his hand to the man. "Can't thank you enough for saving Miss Runyon, Sir."

"*Elle est spéciale*," he said, and then switched to English. "No thanks necessary."

"Indeed she is special. She's going to be my wife. Frenchman are you?"

The man nodded, tipped his cap to Hannah and headed back into the saloon. Hannah and Josiah Parker stared at each other. Her first sight of him stunned her. She remembered in Boston he had always looked so properly dressed when he came to call on her. Now he wore a faded woolen shirt, so dirty its original color was hard to tell, and old trousers held up by rough suspenders. The handsome face she remembered was almost completely covered by hair. After a pause that seemed to last a long time, he reached out to embrace her. She allowed him only a few seconds before pushing him away.

"I am very tired after such a long journey, Mister Parker. Will you take me to the hotel where I can rest for awhile."

"Hotel? Oh, Hannah, there are no hotels in Angels Camp. But you can rest in my cabin."

"That's not proper, Mister Parker."

He gave her a wistful look. "Things are not proper here in Angels Camp the way they are in Boston. I know you'll find my cabin confortable. It's the best I can do."

"The best?" she moaned.

He fetched her trunk from alongside the stagecoach. Hefting it on his shoulder, he led her up a path about a quarter of a mile through a copse of pine trees. Their sweet scent was reassuringly familiar to her. But as they went past several rough-made cabins her fear of what lay ahead grew. *Is his cabin as primitive-looking as these are? She thought. In the middle of a forest? How could he have asked me to give up a Boston townhouse for a wilderness shanty?* When Parker pointed proudly to a large wood frame building partially sided with boards she gasped, "It's not finished. I don't think I can live like this, Mister Parker. Are you asking me to live like a native?"

"Don't worry, it's dry when it rains. The unfinished part will be my carpenter shop. I'll finish the cabin as quickly as I can now you're here and can help out. I've been on the river a lot lately—panning as much gold as I could to have enough to finish building. Oh Hannah, won't it be wonderful with us working together? I am so happy you are here. May I kiss you?"

Hannah gathered her strength and gritted her teeth. She let him brush her cheek with his bearded chin in what passed for a kiss. Then she backed away.

"Will you be shaving off your beard now that I'm here, Mister Parker?"

"I had not planned on that. Will you insist?"

Inside the cabin, it smelled of sawdust and linseed oil.

Hannah told him to keep his distance that evening. She pointed out they were not yet married and that he should sleep on the floor or some other place until they were. And the beard had to go.

She spent a mostly sleepless night, fretful and fully clothed on the hard bed that had wood slats for a mattress. Through the dark hours she wrestled with her thoughts, interrupted frequently by frightening sounds outside the cabin, including an owl on a limb, and what sounded like wild dogs howling off in the distance. She wept at times, thinking the rest of her life might be spent living in a log cabin on a remote mountainside like this one. Finally, she slept fitfully.

In the morning Hannah awoke with a new resolve. She had made this choice, however bad it now seemed. Perhaps her mother had been right, but there was no going back. She determined to make the best of it, and show her mother. Pulling a blanket tight around her shoulders to stop shivering against the morning chill, she assured herself, if this is another of God's tests I will not be found wanting.

"As soon as we are married we can begin to make this shack into a home, Mister Parker, but the beard must come off," she told him over a breakfast of hominy grits he prepared for her.

"The food's plentiful, but there's not much variety," he said when he noticed her inspecting her plate. You do know how to cook, don't you?"

She laughed. It was her first laugh since leaving Boston. "I do indeed, Mister Parker. Did you bring me all the way to California just to cook your meals for you? And I can sew as well. I will make curtains so we can have privacy, and we can buy rugs to cover these dirt floors to keep the dust down. I know you will make handsome furniture for us."

A smile broadened across his face. He swept his hair off his forehead. "I know you will be a perfect wife. I am so lucky to have you. While I stood in the icy stream all day long I fantasized about how our home would look once you added a woman's touch to it, Hannah. Here everyone calls me Parker instead of Josiah so please do so if you like. Soon you will give up your Boston formality. No one is formal here." He waited for a response but Hannah only continued to look at him.

"Before you came I had to balance working on our home with panning enough gold to pay for the wood and supplies. The river is very cold this time of year." He paused, as if to select his words carefully before proceeding. "If you can begin earning gold we'll finish our home in no time. You'll be as comfortable as you were back East. We'll live like a prince and princess when it's all done."

Hannah gave him a questioning look. "Do you expect me to go into the icy river and pick up gold nuggets, or however it is you do that? I don't think that's appropriate woman's work."

He rose from the stool by the stone fireplace where he had been warming and drying his boots. "Oh goodness no, I'd never ask you to do that. Digging the gravel and sifting it through the rocker isn't woman's work. But there are other ways for you to earn your keep."

"How then?"

"The men are busy panning as much gold as they can. They don't spend any time doing the things their womenfolk back home used to do for them, like keeping their clothes clean and mended, cooking their food and tidying their tents. They'd rather pay women to do those things for them. There's a lot of gold for a woman to make washing clothes at the river. The Americans would rather a white woman did that for them than a Mexican or Chilean woman."

"You mean me, Parker?"

CHAPTER 4

1852

EVEN THOUGH DIEGO had been in Angels Camp almost two years, he could not remember ever being as cold as he was at that moment. Unable to feel anything below his knees, and afraid of losing his balance because of the numbness, he maneuvered cautiously toward the edge of the swift-flowing stream. Grabbing onto an overhanging limb of an alder tree to steady himself, he stepped out of the water. Sitting on a large streamside boulder, while a scrub jay marched from side to side on a branch high above screeching at him, he searched both banks of the river, up and down stream, to make sure no one had seen him. He slapped at his thighs to stimulate some warmth. As the blood began flowing back into his legs it felt as if hundreds of knives were stabbing him. He knew he'd been foolish to spend so much time in the icy water, but he had to take as much gold from this gravel deposit as he could before the snowmelt from the higher peaks left it underwater. He had to hurry, no matter how cold the water.

"Hey!" A voice behind him called out, "What are you doing there?"

Diego hadn't expected anyone to come through the forest behind him. He struggled to his feet, jammed his hands into his pocket, gripping the little nuggets. He started moving back from the stream as fast as his aching legs could walk, angling away

Their Golden Dreams

from two men approaching through the trees. He recognized one of them as a man named Blodgett. Still wincing from the pain, and berating himself for not being more guarded, he called back. "Just walking the river." He kept walking. "Looking for color, but found none here."

"Stop a minute, will ya?" Blodgett shouted, hurrying up to him. "Just trying to be neighborly, ya know?" He stopped to catch his breath. "Wanted to make sure you was okay."

"'Course I'm okay. Just walking the river."

"What ya doin' up here?" Blogett's partner asked. "No color up this way, is there?"

"There'd be a crowd here if'n there was, Ike," Blodgett mocked his companion. "The color's downstream aways, closer to camp, right?"

Diego shrugged ignorance. "You're right, I guess. Nothing here I could find. Just thought I give it a try before the runoff starts."

"You find any color around here you be sure to let us know," Ike, taller and younger, but more thinly built than Blodgett, told Diego. "This is our stream now. Shucks, the whole damn state is ours now since the war. So if there was gold to be found a good Californio boy like you would let us know. Wouldn't you?"

Diego fingered the gold deep in his pocket. He feared Blodgett and his buddy could tell it was there. Finally, a spot that looks promising, away from the Yankees downstream, and these two have to come along, he thought. Got to keep it secret. Moving deeper into the trees away from the stream, with Blodgett and Ike keeping stride with him, he stayed silent. Then he stopped to face them. "My father was a Yankee, from New York originally."

"He was?" Blodgett said. "If you ain't a Californio I'll eat my hat. Sure enough you'd be mistook for a damn Sonoran with your dark skin and black hair."

"You hear me?" The younger man walked alongside him now and stared into his face. "The color belongs to us. We'd run all damn foreigners off if there wasn't so damn many, 'specially Sonorans and Chileans."

His legs still aching, Diego walked faster, leading the Americans away from the stream bank. He wanted to keep a tight grip on the gold. It felt to him as if his pocket was bulging, but he pulled his hand away so they wouldn't get suspicious.

"You sure there ain't anything worth diggin' up here?" Blodgett called out, as he and the other man dropped behind.

Late that afternoon Diego and Luc Benard stood at the bar in the Angels Camp Saloon. Tall for a Frenchman, Luc was almost a half a foot taller than his friend. Draining the remains of his whisky in a gulp, he handed the glass over the bar for a refill. Diego barely sipped his drink. He got little pleasure from whisky, but the saloon was the only gathering place in Angels Camp so he met Benard there most days.

Luc spotted one of the French girls across the room, wearing a colorful short dress that revealed a peek of her breasts and her white pantalets, standing beside the faro table. He gave her an admiring smile. Nodding to Diego to follow, he set his glass down on the bar and pushed his way through the crowd of men to her.

"*Un jeu de Faro, Monsieur?*" She winked at him while lightly touching his arm. "Will you take a chance?"

"I don't play. It is a loser's game."

The woman turned to Diego. "And you, *Monsieur? Un jeu?*"

He gave her a smile, but declined.

"I am Miette, *Monsieur.*" She turned back to Luc. "You have the chiseled features and dark look of a Frenchman. I could tell.

I have known many Frenchmen. What is your name?"

"Luc Benard."

"*Bonsoir*, Luc Benard. Have you done well in the diggings?"

"Well enough."

"A game then? Risk a little of your gold."

Luc shook his head.

"Then why did you come to me from the bar, *Monsieur*? I watched."

"I am attracted to beautiful women. Yours is a pretty face in a sea of ugly men. Why did you come to Angels Camp?"

Miette laughed coarsely. "The gold, of course. You are a handsome man, *Monsieur*, but not so bright."

"Of course, the gold." He laughed with her. "A silly question for a woman of your obvious charms."

"The same reason you came, *Monsieur*. And your friend here, too. The reason we all came." She smiled sweetly again, showing the dimple in her cheek, then sighed and shrugged her shoulders. "But I think you are asking why I left France, no? I am not ashamed to say I had no choice, but it has turned out well for me. The *gendarmerie* in Paris offered many young women the opportunity for us to leave." She touched his arm again. "If you find me attractive I could be free later this evening."

"For gold?"

"For gold, *oui*."

"For now I keep all the gold I am able to wrest from the river, Miette."

"Perhaps you will have more than you need some day. Then you will come looking for me, no? I will be here. You came for gold just as I did. You get yours from the river. I get mine from the men at the faro table. We do what we must, isn't that so? In France life was not so simple."

Luc nodded. "Not so simple."

"We came for the gold, but we start new lives." The strong, interrupting voice belonged to a slight man with light brown hair who had joined them. "It's a fresh start here, isn't it? For all of us. We have the freedom to change if we want, don't we?"

"And what is your name, *Monsieur*?"

"Josiah Parker."

"So you think we can start new lives here in the gold diggings, do you?" Miette didn't wait for him to respond. A shadow darkened her pretty face. Her words were sharper now. "For some of us there is no new life, only the same old life we had before, but in a new place." She looked each man squarely in the face, fixing her eyes on them in turn. "Some will get rich. I doubt many. What will you do when the gold runs out, *Monsieur* Parker? I think you will still do the same things you did before you came to Angels Camp."

"Not so, Miss. I am a carpenter. My life will be different. Here I can still be a craftsman."

Miette turned away momentarily to look around the gambling hall before turning back. "I want my life to be different, too—I pray for that—but I think it will not be so different than it was in Paris. We bring our old life with us, like turtles, with old baggage on our backs." She turned to another miner, smiling sweetly again. "*Un jeu de blettes, Monsieur?*"

Luc and Parker looked at each other. "A sobering thought, Parker. Don't you agree? Will you have a drink with us?"

"Thank you, but no, sir. I came in to talk with the proprietor about making new chairs for him to replace ones that have been broken. I must get back to my woman now." He gave Luc a serious look. "But wait. Aren't you the one who rescued my Hannah from the crowd when she first arrived?"

"I am. She looked afraid so I was happy to help her."

"The girl's wrong, you know," Parker told Luc and Diego. "We can always change our lives if we set our minds to it."

"Did you make chairs before you came to Angels Camp?"

"I did." Parker paused. "I see what you are saying, but this is a new world and a new chance for me. Here I can be independent. I can support a wife and family from the work of my own hands."

Luc turned to Diego. "What about you, my friend?"

"My life has already changed. It has nothing to do with the gold. It changed when the war came. Nothing is the same for me now."

"I came from France so my life here is very different. If I return I think it will be much the same as before."

"Are you finding enough gold?"

"I came with a company of Frenchmen. We work together. We're doing well enough."

"You're in the camp down in the hollow then?"

"As far away from Americans as we can get. No offense to you intended."

"None taken, Luc. There are so many French here, almost as many as the Mexicans and Chileans. And you, Diego? Enough color in the streams to fill your pouches?"

Diego hesitated. His hand went to his side to reassure himself the nuggets were still in his pocket. "I will take back any gold I find to our rancho in Santa Barbara. For my mother. It will have to be enough."

"I would like to know more about your country, Luc. I was unaware the French were such good miners."

"Many are, although there is no gold in France. We mine coal, but conditions in France were not good after the Revolution. There were no jobs. Many were begging food on the streets."

"I must get back to my cabin. Hannah is still quite unsettled when she's left alone. I want to marry her, but she's darn fussy. Wouldn't let the *alcade* do it last week. Wants a regular preacher. So we will wait until one comes up from Stockton. A darn inconvenience for me. She says I must sleep on the floor while we wait." Parker grinned, then thought for a moment. "Would you and Diego care to come back to the cabin with me? To talk some more. It is always nice to make new friends. Hannah's a passable cook. Always has a pot of stew going."

Luc Benard gave Hannah a warm greeting as he followed Parker and Diego through the cabin door. She felt as if he were inspecting her with his eyes. But she quickly realized she was doing the same thing to him, so she returned the greeting and thanked him again for his kindness the first day she arrived. He was tall, dark, handsome—all the things young girls in Boston daydreamed about. He had an uncombed mass of dark hair and his pearl gray eyes shone brightly, but it was his manly presence, the way he dominated Parker and the other man that seemed to fill the cabin.

When Parker introduced Diego Austen to her he seemed inconsequential by comparison. Young, probably her own age, maybe younger, and nondescript. He looked much like the other Mexican and Chilean miners in Angels Camp. He greeted her politely, but with little animation.

"These men are new friends. I invited them for dinner. I was hoping you might have some of your delicious biscuits and stew warming on the fire. Is there enough, Hannah? Perhaps a piece of pie, too?"

Hannah took just an instant to shoot him a sharp look. Then her face grew sweetly benign. "Of course, Mister Parker, we'll make do." She gestured to the newcomers. "Make yourselves as comfortable as our humble cabin allows. I'll see to the food."

When the men were seated around the plank table Parker had built, Hannah served a stew of beef chunks, carrots, and onions in crockery bowls, with cold Dutch oven biscuits to sop up the dark gravy. Then she joined them at the table, listening to their discussion and commenting when it seemed appropriate. Parker pumped Luc with questions about life in France.

"In 1848, I was apprenticing in Paris with a *négociant*, a wine merchant you would say." Luc told him. "The business dried up after the revolution and a depression started. I lost my job. So I joined *Le Toison d'Or* looking for some adventure. We pooled our money to come to California. It seemed a more exciting thing to do than returning to my parents' home in Épernay."

Hannah interrupted. "A revolution, you say?"

Luc looked at her and smiled. "You Americans are no strangers to revolution are you? In France we seem destined to keep repeating ours. I suppose we are a fighting people."

"Do you fight for a cause?"

"No, there was a lot of unrest. Times were bad—Crops failed, bread was expensive, there was a drought. The people had no money."

As Luc talked, Hannah watched Diego. He listened, but seemed withdrawn. When there was a pause, she turned to him. "You're very quiet, Mister Austen. Tell us about your life before coming to Angels Camp."

"Since '46 we have lived through difficult times, too."

"Fortunately we are at peace now."

Diego scoffed, showing more emotion than Hannah had seen in him to that point. "You Yankees are at peace, Parker, we Californios have lost our world," he said.

"We must put aside our differences and learn to be one country, Diego."

"The difference is that you Americans now own the country where I was born. You Americans want to take all the gold in these foothill streams for yourselves."

"Have you had trouble with Americans on the river?" Hannah asked him.

"Soon after I got here I learned it was best to find spots on the river away from others. No trouble, ma'am, but we fight with the foreign miners for the scraps."

"Is that why you came? To get your share of the scraps?"

"Not at first, ma'am." Diego looked at Parker and then back to Hannah, searching for the right words. "I came with *vaqueros* from my mother's rancho. We drove a herd of our cattle to Stockton to sell. We had to sell our cattle to pay our debts."

"And you stayed on?"

Diego looked down at the table, as if to avoid Hannah's question.

Luc waited a moment and then interrupted the silence. "It is my fault if you must know, *Mademoiselle*. Diego asked me to bring him to Angels Camp so he could pan for gold."

"The herders left you behind?"

"They didn't know where I had gone. Victoriano—he was head *vaquero*—had no choice." Diego straightened up at the table. More strength came into his voice. "I didn't want to go back right away. I do not blame him for leaving. No, I cannot blame Victoriano at all. He had all the gold from selling the cattle. It was not safe to stay looking for me. My mother needed the *vaqueros* back at the rancho. She needed the gold. He had to leave."

Hannah interrupted Diego before he could say more. "Does your mother know you are here?" When he looked blankly at her, Hannah's face took on a questioning look. "Your mother doesn't even know if you are alive or dead? Is that right?"

Diego gave her a sad look. "I suppose you are right," he said finally, "For now I am on my own. I am old enough to fend for myself. Please do not misunderstand, I miss my mother and do not want her to worry, but I must go my own way for a while. When I return to her I will take all the gold I find here."

"And where is your rancho?"

"Near Santa Barbara."

"I've heard of Santa Barbara. How far is it?"

"A four or five days' ride from here with no cattle to drive." A brighter look came over Diego's face. He sat straighter, as if energized by the thought of home. "It is a wonderful rancho my mother has. It stretches from the ocean, where you can stand on the beach and see the islands, to the base of the mountains where the sun reflects golden light off the rocks in the morning and a pink glow before it sets at night. We have many green valleys of oak and sycamore where our cattle and horses run free. My father was a ship captain who brought her the best horses for breeding from around the world...before he died."

Hannah's eyes looked from Diego to Luc and then back at Diego. "I am sorry to hear you lost your father. I never knew mine. He left my mother before I was born. Sailed for Santa Barbara, but he never returned to her. I wonder if your mother ever knew him."

CHAPTER 5

1852

HANNAH RUNYON AND Josiah Parker were married in late winter when a Methodist minister came to Angels Camp on his circuit of Sierra foothill mining camps. Their married life settled into a routine that saw Hannah taking in laundry from other miners and washing it on the river's edge while Parker panned for gold nearby. Most days the weather was clear, with a sharp chill that reminded her of New England winters, but the Stanislaus River ran icy cold. It numbed her hands as she worked, but took an even greater toll on Parker, who spent hours in the freezing water. Unnoticed at first, he started coughing. Then a fever set in and Hannah urged him to stay off the river and rest for a few days.

"Stay in bed and get some rest," she said one morning in early spring, giving him a concerned look. "You'll feel better when I get back." She opened the cabin door and stood for a moment breathing in the sweet scent of pine. A pair of mourning doves greeted her. Then she headed toward a quiet stretch of the river carrying a basket of soiled clothing under her arm. Her path took her through a grove of old, gnarled oak trees, looking to her like courtly barristers, pleading their cases to one another with outstretched arms. She emerged into an open meadow, newly green from winter rain and dotted about with gooseberry shrubs and flannel bushes bursting into bloom. She was so startled to see a man standing in the field ahead of her she almost dropped the basket.

"Señora Parker," the man called out to her.

Hannah stepped back and let out a breath. "Oh Mister Austen, you've caught me by surprise."

"I didn't hear you approach. I am sorry if I have surprised you, I was hunting my dinner."

"Indeed you have surprised me, Mister Austen. My heart is still racing. But I'm glad it is you and not some stranger." She pointed at the large dead bird he was just picking up by its legs. "What is it you've killed?"

"Wild turkey. Very good to eat."

"I heard no gunshot."

Diego held up his other hand. "This is Yolanda. The vaqueros taught me to hunt with her when I was young."

"Yolanda?"

Diego laughed and held out a slingshot for her to see. Yolanda was intricately carved in the shape of a beautiful young woman. Her voluptuous torso and legs formed the handle and her upraised arms were the two posts to which the rubber band was attached.

She gave a little giggle. "Apparently you learned to use Yolanda well. What will you do with the dead bird?"

"I'll gut it first, then wrap it. It will stay fresh in the stream while I work my claim today. Tonight we'll roast it on a spit. It will be enough for four or five of us at camp."

Hannah walked beside Diego the rest of the way to the stream. Placing the carcass on a rock, he plucked out a few breast feathers. Then, taking a long knife from his belt, he gutted the bird.

Hannah watched him clean the turkey. "I never guessed life here would be...so difficult."

"What did you expect?" Diego wrapped the carcass and set it aside.

"I don't know what I expected. Life here is so primitive. When I lived in Boston I never thought about having to hunt for food. Never saw it being cut up."

"You don't seem suited for this kind of life. Why did you come here, Señora?"

She let her gaze drift out over the river, watching the icy blue water from the snowmelt upstream surge past them, trying to find words to explain. "I don't know," she said looking back at him.

"To marry Parker?"

"Well, of course I came here to marry Parker. I promised him before he left Boston. But there was more, I guess. California sounded exciting. It was an adventure—starting a new life and building a home. But life here is so primitive."

"I haven't seen Parker on the river for a few days."

"He's taken a chill and coughs a lot..." She paused and looked down at the pebbles in the clear water. "I am overwhelmed by everything. I never know what to do."

"You seem very young."

Hannah gave him a piercing glance. "And you're not?"

"I have always been able to care for myself. Ever since my father was killed I have worked with the *vaqueros*. I know about wild things." He gestured at the carcass.

Hannah gave him a playful look. "You've learned much for such a young boy. And now you are on your own, away from your mother."

"Mother has Victoriano," Diego said. Then he realized she was teasing. He stopped talking for a moment to look around. "I don't like it here. I will go home soon. Back to Santa Barbara to my mother's rancho."

"You've been successful though? Found gold, I mean."

"Some. Perhaps I'll leave soon. I will be glad to go."

"When you came to our cabin you seemed angry, Diego."

"I didn't mean to offend you."

"I was not offended, but what is it that angers you?"

"Perhaps you are different. Other Americans come here to plunder our land. The war is done—we are the losers—we must learn to live as a conquered people."

"Is it so hard?"

"Of course it's hard. How would it be if people who spoke a different language captured Boston? Before, when there were only a few Yankee traders, we got along well enough. Ours was a good life, peaceful."

Hannah was thoughtful for a moment. "When we spoke that evening you painted a wonderful picture of Santa Barbara before the war. If there were only a few Americans then perhaps you know a man by the name of Will Thornton?"

Diego stared hard at Hannah a moment and then turned from her and paced along the river's edge as if he were thinking deeply about her question. Abruptly he turned back to her. "No, Señora Parker, I don't know that name."

Hannah shrugged off her disappointment. "I would like to learn more about him. But Diego, the American men here are very polite—they tip their caps and bid me good day."

"Look around you, Señora. There are few Yankee women here so you are respected. But the American men you call polite are greedy. They are determined to take all the gold in our rivers back east with them. They act as if they own it and can do whatever they choose. They try to push us off the streams. When I go back to Santa Barbara perhaps there won't be so many of them. I hope I will live my life as before."

"Oh, Diego, I am sorry for you, but I fear you will never escape Americans now that we're here, not even in Santa Barbara. We are too many. Too aggressive. I think that is in our blood."

Farther down stream Hiram Blodgett stood at the edge of the river where it flowed around a shallow bend near the village. Watching a Kingfisher flying low along the water on the far side, he took his hand off the rocker handle and let out a long sigh. For an instant he thought of home on the banks of the Ohio near his farm.

Coming back to the work at hand he called out to his son-in-law. "Come on, Ike, you're slowing down. Keep that shovel moving. The sun'll be setting soon and we ain't got much to show for the day's work."

"Keep the shovel movin', ya say." Ike's voice showed his tiredness. "My arm's 'bout to fall off from all this shovelin'. All you've done is rock that cradle back and forth all morning." Ike stopped digging in the loose gravel beside the stream and leaned on the shovel handle. He took off his cap and ran his fingers through his damp hair, stopping at one spot to scratch vigorously. "Lord above, Hiram, you musta picked the worst piece of ground in all of California to dig."

"Don't you go pointing at me, son. We're in this together. If'n we want to ever see our womenfolk again we'd better keep digging or move on."

"What I'd give to see my sweet Louisa again, Hiram. I do love your daughter so, but those Frenchy girls is starting to look pretty good to me too. Sooner we make a strike and head back to the farm the better it'll suit me."

"Never thought it would take us this long to get rich. Or that we'd hav'ta work this hard for it."

"You think we're doin' something wrong, Hiram?" Ike dropped the shovel and walked a few yards down the stretch of rocks and pebbles at the water's edge, looking across the river at a group of

Their Golden Dreams

Mexicans working a long tom. "Look at them Mexican greasers downstream." He pointed. "It looks like they're getting' color in every pan they wash."

Hiram took the top of the rocker off. He gathered the heavy pebbles that had collected on the slats into a pan. Kneeling, he carefully dipped water into the pan, swirling it so the dirt and smaller pebbles flowed over the side. "Dang it!" he said, picking out several small grains of gold and putting them into a drawstring leather pouch on his belt, "Hardly enough to buy us a whiskey tonight. You can forget about them *mademoiselles* at the saloon, Ike. They wouldn't give you the time of day with these slim pickings"

"What we gonna do, Hiram?"

"I don't know, son. I truly don't know."

"You said it would be easy in California—'just bend over and pick up the nuggets outta the rivers,' you said. We maybe ain't never gonna get back home, Hiram."

"Don't start on me, boy. I miss my Sarah as much as you miss Louisa."

Ike picked up a small stone and tossed it into the water in the direction of the Mexicans. "When I was in Mexico with old Rough and Ready we'd pick off the Mexicans like shootin' fish in a barrel—it made a soldier proud. Now we got to watch 'em take our gold outta the river. Just look over yonder at 'em. It ain't right. If they wasn't here there'd be plenty of gold for the rest of us. It just ain't right."

"I know that, Ike. We gotta do something. Can't help thinking about that Californio lad we saw upstream awhile back. He acted peculiar. Kept his hand tight in his pocket. I got a feeling he's on to somethin' up there. Maybe we could throw in with him. Three of us working together could wash more gravel than he can alone, for sure. What do you say? Should we talk to him?"

Ike wiped sweat from his brow with the back of his sleeve and picked up the shovel. "Yeah, Hiram, I guess we could. Or maybe we could just push him off the stream and work that spot ourselves."

When they quit the river at dusk the pair made their way to the saloon. With the few grains of gold they had panned they bought shots of whisky and nursed them at a table in a far corner.

Ike set his glass on the table and sat straight, as if he'd had a new thought. "If it weren't for all these Mexicans and Chileans, Frenchies, too, I think we'd be doing fine, Hiram. They're the ones don't belong here. This is our country now, dang it! I fought for that."

"That'll change, Ike. You'll see when this new tax they's talking about gets started. Most foreigners won't find enough to pay it each month."

"It can't come soon enough to please me."

"But you know, Ike, I'm beginning to think maybe the two of us just ain't cut out for this life. Seems as if there's enough gold in California for everyone. Maybe we're just not lucky enough to get our share."

"Hey, ain't that the guy we was talking about just come in? Let's see what he's gotta say for himself."

Ike was out of his chair and pushing through the crowd before Hiram could stop him. "Hello...what's yer name? Me and my father-in-law saw you on the river awhile back. Remember? Come on over and have a drink with us."

"My name is Diego Austen. I'm looking for a friend. I don't want a drink."

"We have a table in the corner. You can watch for him there. Right now we wanta talk with you." Ike put his hand on Diego's shoulder and gave enough pressure that Diego took a step toward the table.

"No thank you, sir. I don't care to have a drink with you." Diego tried to step away from Ike.

"We just want a friendly talk is all. Hiram there wants to get to know you better."

Diego didn't move. His eyes searched around the room.

"See, your friend ain't here yet." Ike guided Diego to the table and pushed him down in a chair.

"I apologize if Ike was rude to you, Austen. That's your name, ain't it? Diego Austen?" Hiram greeted him. "Sometimes he forgets his manners. Sit a few minutes. I am eager to hear how a young man all alone like yourself is getting along."

Diego stared at Hiram for several moments. "Doing well enough, I guess."

"You speak pretty good for a Mexican," Ike told him.

"I am not a Mexican. I was born in California, so was my mother. My father came from New York."

"No offense," Hiram interrupted. "Ike just meant it as a compliment. Didn't you, Ike?"

Ike shot Hiram a quick scowl at being called out.

"That day we saw you up river," Hiram continued without acknowledging Ike, "Did you find the color you was looking for?"

Diego didn't answer.

"We think ya did," Ike said.

"Did you file a claim up there?" Hiram pressed.

Diego stayed quiet for a moment. Then his brow furrowed in a look that might have been worry or fear. He started to get up, but Ike held his arm to keep him sitting. "I keep to myself, Blodgett. I don't tell people what I do. It's none of your affair. Better for me that way."

"We don't care if you've found a big strike. We'd be happy for you. Did you find gold?"

Diego stared at Hiram, then at Ike, but didn't speak.

"We think you did," Ike said again. "Look, Austen, your silence tells us all we need to know. You found gold."

"Not so fast," Hiram warned Ike.

But Ike was not going to be stopped. "We want to help ya get it outta the ground."

"Help me? What do you mean?" Diego's voice rose. "I don't need your help or anyone's help."

"Take it easy, Austen. Ike's not saying you do. We don't want to take anything away from you. But if you've found a big strike, working together we could help you get it out faster."

"Yeah," Ike added. "Two of us shoveling, we could set up a long tom and get the gold before anyone knew." He stared steadily at Diego, his fingers drumming on the tabletop. "If others was to learn of your good fortune they'd be all over that stretch of river."

Diego started to get up from the table again. "I don't need any help. I've got friends who'll work with me if I need them." He stared at Ike. "And help defend my claim if anyone threatens me."

"So you did find color. Sit down! We ain't exactly threatening you, Austen, just tryin' in a neighborly way to show you the danger you might be in if'n you try goin' it alone."

"Thing is, if you try to work your claim alone it might cost you. The new foreign miners' tax is $20 a month. You gotta dig a lot for that. Together we could get it quicker."

"I am not a foreigner! I'm an American, like you. I don't have to pay any tax." Diego's voice was rising. He looked around the room at men crowding in the door, searching for Luc or some escape route. The noise of the saloon was rising fast, with the clinking of bottles and glasses on the bar and the shouts of the crowd around the gambling tables. At one of the faro table he saw Miette chatting and laughing with a group of miners. He caught her eye. She broke away, walking toward the table, giving a big smile as she approached.

Ike watched her come and then turned back to Diego, his narrowed eyes focused, the muscles in his face drawn tight. "You're all alone up there, Austen. Think about all the bad things that could happen to you and no one would know. Hiram and me just want to help you stay outta trouble."

"*Oui, Monsieur*, I am glad to see you this evening." Miette came alongside Diego and put her hand on his shoulder. "A good day at the diggings, I hope. We are having a very nice game of cards at my table and I need more players." She looked at Ike and Hiram. "Such handsome men as yourselves, lucky miners I am sure, should join us to try your luck. What do you say? Come join me."

In an instant Diego was out of his chair before Ike could stop him. He took Miette by the hand and started pulling her away from the table. "I am ready to try my luck with you tonight, if you will show me how to play your card game." Turning to the two men still sitting at the table he said, "I am finished with our conversation," and walked away, thinking it might soon be time to leave Angels Camp.

Hiram and Ike stared at each other.

Several days later, for the third time in the last half hour, Hannah started for the cabin door carrying her basket of dirty laundry, only to stop again, set it down, and return to Parker's bedside. He lay on a damp blanket, sweat beaded on his forehead, his breath rasping in and out, like the sound of wind rustling in the pine trees outside. She picked up a cloth from the table beside him and mopped at his brow.

"Oh, Parker, what can I do for you?" she said in a low, worried voice. "I don't want to leave you today. Let me fetch you a cool drink before I go."

She went out to the cistern to fill the cup with melted snow. Returning, she hovered over him again, putting the cup against his parched lips. He took a sip then motioned it away.

"I'll be all right as soon as this fever breaks." He paused to gather his breath. "I'll be back on my feet in no time. Maybe tomorrow."

"It's been days and you're not getting better. You spent too much time in the icy river." She set the cup down and put her hand to his forehead. She would have frowned, but he was looking at her so she kept her face calm. "Can you reach this cup of water?" she asked. "It's here by the bed."

"I needed gold to buy tools for the furniture shop." He searched for more breath. "For you," he wheezed. "So I could quit the placers."

Parker reached for the cup but dropped it. Hannah picked it up and went back to the cistern to refill it. When she was out of sight of Parker she squeezed her eyes shut, trying not to cry. There was no doctor in Angels Camp, no medicine and he was getting worse. She forced down her panic and went back inside.

"I'm going into the village to see if I can find some elderberry tea. It will help you feel better." She went out and started walking as fast as she could toward the small collection of wood and canvas buildings that was the town. As she left she heard him cough again inside the cabin.

Arriving at the small general store, she searched the stacked crates and barrels for the tea or anything that might ease Parker's suffering. She was desperate. It showed on her face.

"Mademoiselle, *s'il vous plaît arrêter*. Please." A familiar voice called from behind her. Hannah quickened her steps out the door, but the voice caught up with her outside. "I saw your tears, *Mademoiselle*. Are you all right?"

"It is Missus Parker now." Hannah started to walk away.

"*Madame, Je suis dèsolè*. I didn't know. I have not seen you since our coach ride from Stockton." Miette put her hand on Hannah's shoulder to restrain her. "You are upset. Let me help."

"My husband is sick. I am afraid he will die. In Boston I could find medicines, here I don't know what to do."

"I am sorry. You must be strong. Have faith. Trust in your God."

"How can a woman like you talk to me of God?" She spat the words at Miette.

"You think so poorly of me?"

Hannah didn't answer. The two women stared at each other. Even in the midst of her anguish, Hannah couldn't help admire Miette's dark beauty, but at the same time she was repulsed.

Miette smiled meekly. "I am nothing in your eyes, *Je sais*, but *Mon Seigneur* doesn't hate me, even if you do. He understands."

"Living the life you do?"

Miette brushed away the curls the breeze had blown across her face, but didn't budge from her stance in front of Hannah. "What life would you choose for me, Madame?"

"What you do is not proper." Hannah stopped again, with tears flowing down her cheeks now. "I am sorry for what I just said. What you do is not my affair. I am so scared Parker will not live, Miette. I don't know what I am saying. He is so sick."

"In what way is he sick, Madame?"

"He can barely breathe. He coughs and wheezes. Sometimes he coughs blood. I am sorry for the way I talked to you, Miette... but I am afraid."

"It is all right. Others do the same. Perhaps if you gave your husband several sips of whisky it would cut through whatever is clogging his throat, he might breathe easier."

Hannah started to dismiss the idea, then reconsidered. "Perhaps," she said and stopped again, looking at Miette less harshly, seeing a spark of sincerity in her amber eyes. "I am scared I will be left here alone. I should do something—I am the only one who can—but I don't know what. Before someone has always taken care of me."

"This is a harsh world. Your man may die, you know, but you will survive. I have been alone all my life, but I survive. My parents died of cholera when I was little. I lived on the streets of Paris and begged for bread. I learned to care for myself."

"How awful!"

"It was bad. Nuns took me in, but that was no better. They used me to beg for food and for their own pleasures. I ran from the convent. With God's love and a comely face I learned how to survive. You will, too, Madame. Your man is in God's hands now, but you must go forward wherever your life leads you as best you can, as I have done."

Josiah Parker died early that evening as Hannah sat at his bedside, tears rolling down her cheeks. So consumed was she by her fear of being alone, she hardly noticed when his rough breathing stopped. The whisky Miette recommended had little effect. His body was simply too weak from fighting the infection and stopped trying. For the rest of the night and well into the dawn Hannah stayed beside him, sobbing quietly from time to time, consumed by her thoughts. She wallowed in the feeling it had been her fault. As the reality of his death sank in, her self-pity turned to anger. So that no one else would ever hear, she cursed him for abandoning her. And she cursed the cold unfriendly world closing in around her. She cursed herself. When her cursing stopped her fear took over again.

CHAPTER 6

1852

FOLLOWING PARKER'S DEATH Hannah lived in a dense fog of grief, so the women in Angels Camp wrapped their loving arms around her. They took charge of all the arrangements. They asked one of the miners, previously a Presbyterian minister in Rhode Island, to conduct a simple graveside service. Other men were enlisted to help lower the wooden box that held Parker's remains into the grave they had dug on a hillside overlooking the river. Then they left Hannah to the women and went back to prospecting on the river. It was not the first man they'd buried and they knew it wouldn't be the last. The women helped Hannah back to her cabin. She sat alone on a pine bench just outside the door listening to the doves, not knowing what to do next.

A few days later Luc Benard found her walking in the grove of sturdy oak trees down toward the meadow. "I see you're alone, Hannah. Do you wish company or should I go away?"

It took several seconds before she realized someone was talking to her. She turned slowly and saw him standing just a few feet away.

"Say the word and I will leave you."

"No. Please stay. I really don't want to be alone." She stared at Benard. "I am so lonely."

"It is a terrible thing to lose someone so close so suddenly."

"Have you lost a loved one, Mister Benard?"

"Please call me Luc." He smiled warmly and took a step closer to her. "I have. A French girl who was to be my bride."

"A terrible time," she said.

"A terrible time," he echoed.

She stayed silent, looking around the oaks. On the far edge of the clearing a black-tailed doe stood like a chiseled stone statue watching them, with only her ears twitching. "I suppose. It haunts me already that I am having trouble remembering what he looked like," she said. "We were apart for almost two years and I have been here less than a year."

Luc didn't respond. They stood together in silence a few minutes.

"Was it the same with your intended?"

"The same. I try so hard to form her picture in my mind, but it's never quite clear to me. I blamed myself for not loving her enough."

"Not enough," Hannah agreed. "Tell me about her. What was her name?"

"Claudine. She was the daughter of the merchant I was apprenticed to. Sixteen. Blond hair and bright blue eyes. A beautiful girl."

"So you do still see her in your mind, Luc. How did she die? If I am not being too personal."

"During the riots. She was always a very daring girl who took many risks. She wanted to see the fighting on Rue de Rivoli. She went too close." He paused to take in a breath and steady his voice. "She was hit in the head by a cobblestone someone aimed at a soldier."

"How horrible!"

"Yes, horrible. That's the picture that stays in my head. It won't go away. I was standing beside her, but I could do nothing.

I can still see that stone hitting her."

"I don't know what to do, Luc." When she looked again the doe had vanished into the trees. "What did you do when Claudine died?"

"I came here."

After that day, Luc visited her regularly. Their conversations were simple ones and went in no specific direction, but he was easy to talk with and helped salve her grief. One afternoon he saw her inside the cabin through the panes of a window Parker had installed for her. He knocked softly on the door.

"Come in," she said, showing him the brightest face he'd seen on her since Parker's burial. "I have just baked a berry pie; I picked the wild berries this morning. Would you like to have a slice with me?"

"Indeed, I am very fond of berry pies."

She cut a generous slice for him. They sat facing each other at the big table.

"I hope it's good."

After taking his first bite, Luc beamed his appreciation. "It is quite delicious. It reminds me of the berry pies our cook made when I was growing up in Épernay. You are a good pie maker."

"Parker thought so. It's about the only thing I know how to make really well."

They ate without further conversation. When he finished, Luc put his fork down on the tin plate. "Have you given any thought to what you will do now?"

"I don't know what to do. I can't think. Nothing makes any sense to me."

"Are you thinking about returning to your family in Boston?"

"I could. But there really isn't much reason for me to go back."

"Why is that?"

"My mother and I don't get along all that well. My stepfather and I are not close."

"Your real father?"

Hannah laughed. "I never knew him. He left my mother before I was born." She shrugged her shoulders in a gesture of despair. "I don't have any place to go really." She dabbed at a tear in the corner of her eye with her finger. "It seems I am always alone."

"You'll stay here then?"

"Perhaps for awhile. Parker had a little gold—enough for a few months—he was going to use it to finish his carpenter's shop. After that I don't know. I certainly don't plan on washing other people's dirty clothes the rest of my life."

Luc nodded his understanding. With his finger he scooped some of the berry juice off the plate and sucked it into his mouth. "Awfully good," he said. "Most of the miners in Angels Camp haven't had anything as good as this to eat since they left home."

Hannah rose from the table. "I'll cut you another piece then. If we don't eat it the pie will just go bad."

"Does it take a lot of work to make a pie like this?"

"Oh no, no work at all really. Gathering the berries takes the most time."

"A lot of the men would pay you some of their gold to have a piece of pie that reminds them of home, like yours reminds me of Épernay."

Hannah brought the new slice to the table. "Really?"

"I'm sure. You could serve them a slice at this big table. Maybe they'd stop by in the morning before they head to the river or after they're done in the afternoon."

"That would be a lot of work."

"Yes. A lot of work. But it wouldn't be as hard as scrubbing clothes on the rocks in the river, and likely bring in more gold.

Maybe not a lot, but enough to keep you living comfortably."

"You really think so?"

"I do."

She gave an awkward little laugh. "That's quite an idea. I'll have to think about it."

❧

Soon after she opened her pie cafe, word of Hannah's delicious wild berry pies spread through Angels Camp like a mountain wild fire on a windy afternoon. Luc brought his companions from *Le Toison d'Or* to her cabin to taste them. They told others on the river. She was soon overwhelmed by the gold that poured in. Just as Luc had predicted the miners shared with each other their memories of life back home. She had to hire Concepción, a Mexican woman, to gather the berries while she spent hours baking them in the horno oven outside the cabin.

On a warm, early summer afternoon, as she bustled around the large front room of the cabin, converted now into a small cafe area, serving her customers, she saw Miette standing at the door. The spring breeze tossed her black curls about her face and shoulders. Thinking the beautiful young French woman might be there to stir up trouble, Hannah watched her apprehensively.

"*Vous avez une belle petite patisserie, Madame,*" Miette said coming to stand in front of her. "I have heard many good things from the men about your pies. I came to see for myself. And to ask you to hire me."

"Hire you?" Hannah was taken aback and stammered. "You came to ask me for a job?"

"*Oui.*"

"You have a job at the saloon."

"*Oui.* But I can see that you need help and I want to help you."

"What would you do?"

"Whatever you asked of me. I could collect the berries for you or serve the pies to the men or wash tin plates. Whatever you needed doing."

"The wild berry season will end soon, Miette. I don't know that I will need any help when that happens."

"I know it will end soon, so we will have to find new fruits to bake pies with."

"We?" Hannah paused. "What do you know about baking pies?"

"Nothing, Madame. You could teach me to bake them. What I know is that the men crave your wild berry pies and the pleasure of coming here with their friends to eat them. They talk about this at the saloon all the time. You must surely know you cannot stop when this berry season ends. So we should find new fruits, other berries, to bake in pies. I can show you I am a hard worker so you will make me your partner."

Hannah was nonplussed. "My partner, you say?" She stared at Miette thoughtfully. The young woman's amber eyes shone with intensity, her jaw was firmly set, giving a fine definition to her pursed lips as she returned Hannah's look. There was no conceit or self-consciousness in Miette that Hannah could see. She was the same pretty, dark French woman she had met on the stage from Stockton, still beautiful and self-possessed. She sensed Miette could likely accomplish whatever she set her mind on. Hannah felt a touch of jealousy, but thought she could use someone like that.

"It would not work, Miette. I am sorry. I cannot have my customers coming here to see you for..." She couldn't find the right words.

"You think I would solicit them? Or take them away to the saloon? Is that it?"

"Well, yes, I do."

"I don't want that life anymore. I want to make a new one." Miette looked down as she spoke. "I thought you would help me, being the Christian woman you say you are. Perhaps I was wrong."

"But wouldn't the men expect you to... entertain them? What will they think if they see you here?"

"I don't care what they will think. I will leave the saloon and never go back to it again, or that kind of life, if you will give me this chance, Madame. Do you really think that I do what I have done because it is what I want for my life? Every day I have spent on this earth I have done only what I had to do to live. You can never imagine the shame of that life."

Hannah didn't know how to respond. She looked at Miette dumbfounded.

"I thought you might give me a chance to start again. I see from the look on your face I misjudged you, Madame. I am sorry, I will leave you." Miette started for the door.

Hannah was stunned. She wasn't sure what to do, but she felt as if a turning point in her life was abruptly upon her. "Wait!" she called out to Miette.

As she had each day since opening what Miette now called her *petite patisserie*, Hannah made sure all was in order before the afternoon rush of men descended on her cabin. She was pleased with the progress her little business was making. Hannah had arranged with Stockton merchants to have tablecloths and napkins shipped from mills back east, and Miette had created a garden-like setting outside the back of the cabin, with newly built wooden tables to accommodate the crush of men who came each afternoon.

"Madame, you must try this new pie. Concepción has just finished baking the first batch," Miette interrupted Hannah's inspection.

"Are you sure about this? The men like our berry pie so much, do you think adding wild strawberry is a good idea?"

"*Oui*, Madame, a very good idea. For a while they will have a choice. The blackberries will soon be gone for the year so we must find other berries for them as the summer goes on. The Miwok woman who showed me where the wild strawberries grow has taught Concepción how to add honey to sweeten the pies so we don't need to buy as much sugar at sixty cents for two pounds at the market."

"We'll know soon enough. You are a good business woman, Miette."

"Just think how happy they will be when they have a choice of pies."

"Exciting to watch our little business grow, isn't it?"

"Trust me, Madame, it will grow bigger and bigger, you will see. And the gold rewards us for our efforts."

While they talked, a lone man approached the women through the pine grove surrounding the cabin. With a quick nod to Miette, he came straight to Hannah and doffed his sweat-stained cap.

"A fine afternoon, is it not, Missus Parker?"

"Fine indeed. What brings you here so early?"

"I don't know if you know me by name," the man said. "I am Levi Shaw. I've been coming here regularly. I can't get enough of your wonderful berry pies. I've come to talk with you privately, if I might?"

"I'm pleased you like the pies we serve, Mister Shaw. Feel free to say whatever is on your mind." Hannah nodded to Miette. "Perhaps you could check on Concepción."

Hannah looked Shaw over closely while he gathered his thoughts. A man in his forties, with nondescript features, and medium, dark brown hair, he wore typical miner's clothes, showing rips and tears and a pressing need to be laundered. But the feature that immediately grabbed Hannah's attention and wouldn't let go, like some evil spirit trying to possess her, was Shaw's unbearable odor. It was as if he were carrying dead fish in his trousers. The stench forced her to step back from him.

Shaw paid no attention. He took off his cap and held it with both hands. Smiling did not seem comfortable for him, but he tried to force one on his stoic face. "I'm a Maine man, Missus Parker. I'm not given to beating around the bush and making fancy talk. I was a friend of Parker and I am sorry for your loss. But I will come right to the point. I've come to propose marriage to you."

Hannah stayed silent and looked away, trying to stifle a laugh and keep a straight face without gagging on his smell.

Shaw read her silence as an invitation to continue. "You are a beautiful young woman. It is not right for you to be alone in these hills with all these men. You need someone to protect you and your nice little business, and I'm the man to do it."

"I'm flattered..." Hannah struggled to get control of the absurd thoughts racing through her head that she would have to live out her life always inhaling Levi Shaw's horrendous odor or raise his foul-smelling children. "It is not possible. I hardly know you, Levi. I am surprised I never met you when Parker was alive if you were such a friend. Perhaps you are joking with me."

Shaw took two steps closer, forcing Hannah to take three steps back when his putrefying smell engulfed her.

"Not joking at all, Hannah—may I call you Hannah? I've watched the men come here mornings and afternoons for some weeks now. They bring their pouches of gold dust and silver coins to add to your stash. It might not be safe for you. I can help you guard your gold. Together we could build your business."

"Guard my gold, you say? Is it my gold you want to marry or me, I wonder? Either way my answer is no. I will not marry you."

As Shaw confronted her, still standing too close for her to breathe comfortably, Hannah watched a group of French miners arrive and take seats at their usual tables. Luc was with them. He waved to her but didn't approach. Other miners, mostly Americans, were drifting in to their regular seats.

Hannah acknowledged Luc with a smile and quick wave.

"Surely you are not letting that swarthy-looking Frenchman court you, are you, Hannah?"

"That is not your concern. I have given you my answer, Levi. I think our conversation is done."

"He is so dark, I wonder about him. He could be... Caribbean for all you know."

"Levi, you need a bath! I cannot imagine any woman marrying you. You smell awful, please go away! Sit with your friends if they'll have you, and eat some of our pies. My answer is no and no again. You are the tenth man who has proposed to me and I have refused all of them. I do not want to get married, I am very capable of taking care of myself, besides you smell terrible."

Shaw stood in front of her several moments longer, as if standing there would change her mind. Finally, he replaced the cap on his head and walked off.

Luc came toward her. Darkly handsome, she thought, not Caribbean.

"*Bonjour, ma cher.*"

"I am especially glad you came this afternoon, Luc, where have you been?"

"I went down to Stockton with Diego and a few of my companions for a couple of days. I have missed you."

"It is good you're back. We have a new pie for you to sample."

"My mouth is watering. Tell me."

"We have strawberry pies now to go along with the wild berry we have been serving."

He grinned from ear to ear. "In France we look forward to wild strawberries every spring. I am sure my friends will be as eager to taste them as I am."

Over her shoulder, she saw Miette coming from the large new horno oven Hannah had asked some Mexican men to build in back of the cabin to meet the growing demand for pies. She carried two trays, each with eight slices of strawberry pie. She set one tray down in front of Levi Shaw and the other American miners, and the other on the Frenchmen's table. Then she collected the gold and retreated to pick up more pies Concepción was taking from the oven.

Luc returned to his table and grabbed a slice of pie. "*Magnifique*," he shouted after he took his first bite.

"*Fraises, très bon*," one of the men at the table chorused, jumping to his feet. Enthusiastic praise from the other Frenchmen followed. "It is a taste of home," another shouted. "*Merci, Madame, merci beaucoup*."

The Americans watched the Frenchmen happily stuffing pie in their mouths, with strawberry juice running down their chins. They looked down at their own pies. Shaw was the first of them to rise from the table.

"Where are the berry pies we've always had?"

"The season is growing late for them," Hannah explained. "We now have a better supply of strawberries. We will offer other fruit pies as the summer progresses."

"We want our wild berry pies, not strawberry."

Other Americans echoed his words. "We want the berry pies we've always had. Bring us wild berry pies," they began to shout.

Hannah looked helplessly at Miette, who had just returned with more strawberry pies and was distributing them to all the tables.

"Madame Parker must bake what is available," Luc shouted to the Americans. "Be reasonable! Enjoy these new pies."

"Wild berry pies, wild berry pies," the American men began to chant. "We want wild berry pies."

"You cannot tell us what pies to eat." Shaw glared at Luc across the space separating them. We will have the pies we want."

Luc laughed at him. "You expect Hannah to produce pies from fruit that is not available, as if she could magically do such a thing. I say again, be reasonable. These strawberry pies are every bit as good as the wild berry pies. Sit down and enjoy them."

"I will not eat French pies," Shaw shouted back. "You Frenchmen cannot tell us what to eat." He glared at Luc across the space that separated them. "If you like wild strawberries so much, here." He picked up a piece of pie and flung it across the space separating him from Luc. It splattered against his chest, sending a spray of strawberry juice in his face.

Almost immediately the other American miners jumped up and began throwing their pies at the French miners, shouting, "Wild berry pies! Wild berry pies!"

For a brief moment the startled Frenchmen kept their seats as pies flew at them at all angles from the American tables. Then they were on their feet, returning the Americans' pies and adding their own to the melee. "If it's a war you want..." they shouted.

Hannah and Miette did a quick retreat into the cabin, shutting the door behind them.

CHAPTER 7

1852

DIEGO STOOD AT the rail of the small steamer in the gathering darkness of San Francisco Bay. He had left Angels Camp for good days before, riding down to Stockton with Luc, missing the pie war between the French and American miners. With his knapsack slung over his back, he gauged the distance to the wharf, getting ready to jump to it. The sky was clear, with just a slight chill. An occasional cloud obscured the quarter moon that shone dully on the surface of San Francisco Bay.

"Steady, lad" the deckhand cautioned. "Don't jump too soon. Don't wanta lose ya this close. Comin' from Stockton, ay. Successful in the diggings?"

"Did well enough."

"Why did you leave?"

"Had my fill of it."

Diego leapt onto the wharf. The heavy weight of gold in his knapsack unbalanced him so he had to reach out to grab hold of a wooden post to keep from falling back into the narrow band of water between ship and wharf. As he pulled himself to safety his jacket caught on a splinter. He heard it rip.

A young man standing on the wharf helping to secure the steamer reached out to steady him. "Lucky it was only your jacket not yer leg," he said. "Welcome to San Francisco, my name's Pádraig."

"Thanks for your help. Almost fell in. Ripped my jacket, too."

He winced looking at the damage. "Where can I find a meal and room for the night, Pádraig?" he asked, looking at the City spread out before him at the end of the wharf.

"There's plenty of places, friend. Just head up to Portsmouth Plaza. You might try the City Hotel on Kearny Street at Clay. Clean enough, I guess, and won't cost ya much. The food's passable."

"Know where I might get this jacket mended?"

"In fact, I do know a woman who sews all sorts of things for people. Too late tonight though." Pádraig thought a moment. "If you come by here in the morning I'll walk you down there to her."

Diego agreed then hurried off the wharf onto a muddy street and headed toward the cluster of lights he took to be Portsmouth Plaza where he found the hotel. He secured his night's lodging and then found the dining room, crowded with men, talking loudly and attacking heaping platesful of hot food. There were no empty tables, but in one corner a man sat alone with a vacant chair opposite him. Diego hesitated then went toward him. "May I?" he said, pointing to the chair."

"*Mais oui*," the man answered. "Please join me." He gave Diego a jovial smile. At least forty and darkly complexioned, the man had large dark eyes under a heavy brow in his round face, and a thick, bulbous nose. He wore dark green trousers with a brown jacket and tan-colored vest. A red cravat was tied at his neck.

Almost immediately a waiter stood at Diego's shoulder.

"You can't go wrong with the mutton chops and boiled potatoes," his tablemate told him. Diego nodded to the waiter.

"Are you alone?"

Diego nodded again.

"Tels un jeune home!"

Diego looked perplexed

"*Je suis désolé*—I apologize" the man said. "I am Ramón d'Bouviere, pleased to meet you. And what is your name?"

Diego told him.

"In French I said you are such a young man to be traveling alone."

Diego shrugged again. "I know only a little French."

"You do not say much, do you?" D'Bouviere laughed heartily. "If you do not want to talk with me it is all right. Only say so."

Diego looked up abruptly. "No sir, I mean no disrespect."

"What is it brings you to San Francisco, *mon ami*? You have left the gold fields, no?"

Diego chewed on a hard potato until he could swallow it. He took his time, looking around at the room full of loud-talking men before turning back to d'Bouviere. "I went to the diggings with a herd of cattle from Santa Barbara. Now I'm here to see the City."

"You found gold then? From the placers?"

Diego set his fork down on the table and with his hand checked that the knapsack he'd hung on the back of his chair was safe. He looked at the man for several seconds, deciding to watch his words. "Some. Not too much."

D'Bouviere laughed. "What a wonderful land that gives up its riches to those who only need to bend over to pick them up."

Diego smiled and kept chewing a tough piece of mutton.

"Well, I am on my way to Pacific House for a game or two of chance when I finish my dinner. It is a gentleman's establishment. Would you like to accompany me? Being new to the city you will be amazed at the diversions you can find there."

"I would like to."

When Diego finished eating d'Bouviere took his broad-brimmed hat from the floor beside his chair and rose from the table. Leaving the hotel, he led Diego along Kearny and Washington Streets, alive with the noise of men coming from restaurants and gambling saloons around the moonlit plaza. He knocked on the door of a wood-frame three-story house and waited. Inside Diego heard music and voices. When the door opened a footman in green livery with white stockings greeted them. Diego's gaze swept past the man to the large interior room beyond. Decorated in red and gold tones, it had heavy damask drapes and gilded tables next to plush upholstered chairs and settees. Men and a few women talked in low voices. Some stood by a pianoforte singing along with the music. Dozens of candles in a crystal chandelier illuminated the room. Diego hesitated, but d'Bouviere urged him inside.

A woman in a silk dress in the tight-fitting Chinese style that clung to her hips, with a split up one thigh, and a high neck, approached them. Her arms were bare and her skin was the color of coconut husks. Diego couldn't stop staring at her.

"*Monsieur* d'Bouviere, good evening. I was beginning to think we might not see you tonight." The woman greeted them with a smile that showed white teeth framed by brightly painted lips.

"Never miss a chance to twist the tiger's tail," d'Bouviere answered. "I've brought a new friend with me this evening. This young man is Diego. He just arrived in the City."

The woman extended her hand. "Welcome, Diego." Then she took d'Bouviere by the arm and led them to an adjacent room where faro tables were already crowded with players. "If you are a friend of *Monsieur d'Bouviere*, you are welcome in my house," she told Diego as they walked. "May I take your jacket and knapsack? They will be quite safe with my footman while you're here."

Diego tightened his grip on the knapsack.

"You are quite welcome to keep them then," she said, bowing

slightly. Straightening, she looked at him, laughed gently, and walked off.

Diego held back when d'Bouviere pushed through the crowd gathered around the faro tables. Through the smoke of the onlookers' cigars, he watched the game. D'Bouviere was fearless in the way he played. He won more than he lost, picking up small sacks of gold dust or nuggets from the banker's pile when he did, bringing them to his side of the table. The onlookers applauded their favorite players enthusiastically, and were quick to shame losers, but they watched d'Bouviere with awed respect.

Diego soon tired of watching. He walked back toward the main room and stood in the doorway studying the men and women there. Almost immediately his eyes fixed on a young woman standing beside the pianoforte. Catching him looking, she smiled and beckoned for him to join her. She was wearing a tight-fitting gown and a long mauve overskirt with delicate white *fleurs de lis* embroidered on it. The white bodice, with drawstrings in the front, revealed her bare shoulders and a modest peek of her girlish breasts. Ringlet curls in her long, auburn hair framed her face and hung down the back of her neck. Diego was struck by her beauty and started toward her.

"I am Nanette," she said when Diego stood beside her. "I arrived from Paris just this week. Come sit with me, *Monsieur*." Taking his hand, she led him to a quiet corner. "We will sit and talk awhile and sip champagne, no?" Nanette gave him a warm smile that parted her lips and showed dimples in her rouged cheeks. Her dark brown eyes dazzled him. She pointed him to a red velvet couch and settled herself close beside him. He felt her thigh pressing against him.

She signaled a nearby waiter and almost immediately a bottle of champagne and two crystal goblets on a silver tray arrived on the table in front of them.

"Have you been in a fight?" Nanette asked as she handed him one of the goblets, showing him another of her oversized smiles. "I see your jacket is ripped. It is so manly to fight."

Diego grimaced and shook his head.

"You ripped it in gold fields then?"

Diego wasn't sure what to say. His hand patted the knapsack beside him on the couch, on the side away from Nanette.

She smiled and placed her hand softly on his shoulder. Waving off the waiter, she took the bottle of champagne from the tray with her other hand and poured it into his glass. "You must pay now," she said softly in his ear.

He opened his knapsack with care and slowly took out a small pouch. Untying the drawstrings, he poured a small amount of gold dust onto the tray and looked up at the waiter who continued to stand there looking down at the gold.

"Let me show you." Nanette gently took the pouch from Diego's hand and added a generous amount of gold to the tray. "I see you have done well, Monsieur. Let us toast to your good fortune. And to mine for having you as my new friend. What is your name, sir?"

The shock of parting with so much gold was dimmed by Nanette's beauty. He could not stop looking at her. It made him weak-kneed. His groin ached.

Diego looked at the bubbles rising in her gold-rimmed goblet as she touched it to his. He followed her lead, raising his glass to his lips. The effervescence of the champagne tickled in his nose and startled him. He hoped she hadn't noticed.

"You are pleased with me?" she asked, setting her glass down and touching his cheek.

He was at a loss for words.

"If you have more gold we could go upstairs to my room together," she whispered. "There are many things I could teach you."

Overwhelmed by his conflicting feelings, it was all he could do to look at Nanette, even though he thought she was one of the prettiest women he had ever seen. He was giddy with anticipation and scared at the same time.

Nanette sensed his hesitation. "This is your first time, Diego, No? Don't worry, I will be very gentle with you."

He rose from the couch, holding his knapsack in front of him. "Sorry, I cannot stay." His voice was strained and hoarse. He stammered. "You are a beautiful girl, Nanette." Looking around the room, trembling, he was afraid of losing his will if he looked into the depths of her brown eyes. "I cannot be with you. I am sorry, I must leave." He started toward the door.

She bounced up off the couch and gave him a piercing look of scorn. "*Pourquoi*, Diego? Oh, *triste jeune home*, I am so disappointed in you." Her face was flushed. She thrust her hands on her hips. "I thought we could be lovers. I was ready for you tonight. When you realize your foolishness and decide to come back you may not find me so available. Think twice before you leave me, sir. Many men in San Francisco desire to be with me. You are making a big mistake, Monsieur." She turned her back on him and stormed out of the room.

Diego met Pádraig at the wharf the next morning. A light easterly breeze was chasing the fog back over the western hills, the Bay was starting to come alive with boats moving in all directions.

"Glad you remembered," Diego greeted him. "I'd like to get my jacket mended as quick as possible."

"Happy to do it for ya. I make my livin' helping strangers

find their way around the City. Used to meet all the arriving steamers, but now just once in a while. It was a bit of luck we met up last night. I let some of the other lads work the wharves and pay me a share of the tips they get. We don't have far to go, Emma's shop is just a walk down Dupont Street to Pine."

When they entered the small dress shop, Pádraig greeted Emma Laughten and her teenage daughter, Sophie, like close friends.

"Good morning, Emma, I have brought ya a new customer."

"New customer, is it?" Emma Laughten replied. She was seated on a plain wooden bench with a sewing table beside her. "It's a new set of fingers I be needin'." She set the needle in her hand and the dress she'd been embroidering aside and combed her fingers through strands of dull, red-brown hair streaked with gray. "Look at these hands o' mine!" she complained, but let Pádraig know by the warmth of her smile she was glad to see him. "Raw they are from all the work I do. Step back, both of ya. Can't ya see I need some light?"

"Diego here has ripped his jacket."

"Take it off. Let me look." Right away she found the seam and sorted through a box of threads beside her, looking for a close color match. "Why isn't your ma mending it?" She asked as she threaded a needle.

"She's not here," Diego told her.

"On your own, are ya? Sophie, come here," she called out.

Sophie Laughten rose from the table in the corner of the room where she had been cutting silk fabric off a long bolt and came to her mother's side.

Diego took her in with a quick, guarded look. On the skinny side, he decided. Fair complexioned and pale blond hair, almost straw color. Nothing like Nanette. But she did have a sweet face, he had to admit.

Sophie Laughten smiled at Diego and he returned it, but she

gave Pádraig a lingering look. "What is it you want, Mother?" She asked.

"I'll be wantin' more tea if you could fetch me a cup."

Working steadily, Emma finished repairing the jacket. She stood from the bench and handed it back to Diego.

"*Gracias, señora.* It looks as if it had never ripped."

Diego paid Emma and thanked her again.

"Now your jacket's mended I'd be happy to show ya around the City," Pádraig told him. Together they headed back toward Central Wharf at the foot of the plaza. "She's a beaut, ain't she?" He pointed to the side-wheeled vessel anchored several hundred yards off the wharf. "That's the Pacific Mail that came in a couple of days ago."

Diego strained to see the beauty. "I don't know much about steamships. Never been on one." He stared at the flotilla of abandoned ships in the bay for several minutes. "My pa was a ship's master," he told Pádraig, coming back from the end of the wharf. "Sailed all over the world but never took me along. The trader he sailed for left my mother with a baby after Pa died."

"What a terrible thing—leave a woman like that."

"Funny, a woman in Angels Camp knew about him. Said he left her mother, too."

"Bet ya miss your da."

"'Course I do. Most every day. I never really got to know him though. He was away from our rancho so much. I was just nine or ten, when he got killed by a horse."

"I sailed the ocean just once my own self. Came to New York from Ireland in '44."

"Alone?"

"Sure enough. Weren't no other way. My ma and da couldn't feed me so they sent me off. Lived in Dublin awhile. Worked my way to New York on a packet ship—no great beauty she was, I can tell ya, not like the steamer out there."

"How'd you manage? On your own, I mean."

"You do what ya haveta to survive. In New York I lived on the streets. Was a runner for some of the politicians. A volunteer fireman. I'm a volunteer fireman here, now."

"Come to California for the gold?"

"No, before that. When the war started, Colonel Stevenson—one of the politicians I was telling ya about—he formed a regiment to come out to fight in the war. Took a lot of us street boys in the Bowery with him. Wanted us off the streets, I reckon. We didn't do much fightin', just a bit down in Lower California. When the war was over we were left here. Turned out to be a pretty fair bargain for me, what with men coming from all over for the gold. I've been making a living on the wharves ever since. How about you?"

"Did well enough in the diggings, but it wasn't much to my liking." Diego pursed his lips, thoughtful for a moment, then he changed the subject. "You know Pacific House, Pádraig? I met a girl there last evening. She wanted to take me to her room, but I ran off."

Pádraig looked at him, grinning broadly. "Pacific House, yer sayin'? Pretty hoity-toity place, ain't it? Too rich for me, I'm sure. Why'd you run off? Didn't ya have the gold?"

"I didn't want to leave. She was a beautiful girl. Gave me the chills she was so pretty. But I got scared. I was carrying all my gold from the diggings in my knapsack. Taking it home for my mother. I thought the girl was going to steal it so I left her."

"You ought to keep your gold in a money belt. That way its always with you."

Diego nodded agreement, but his thoughts were still on Nanette. "Can't get her out of my mind. Think I'll stay in the City till I can be with her again. I got the gold."

Their Golden Dreams

Diego went back to Pacific House that evening but the green-liveried footman chased him away, saying he was no longer welcome there. Several days after that he tried again to see her, telling the footman to take the message to her that he was sorry for his poor manners and now had plenty of gold for her. The response had been the same each time. "Mademoiselle Nanette does not wish to ever see you again."

Finally, with several ounces of gold, he bribed the footman to let him in the door. Once inside he immediately saw her seated on one of the red velvet couches in the large room, gossiping with several other women. He rushed up to her.

"I have brought gold, Nanette, a lot of gold. I want to give it to you if you will take me to your room as you promised that first night. Please Nanette, I have thought of nothing but your beautiful face, your body, since the night I acted so foolishly."

The other women in the group tittered happily at Diego's pleading, but at a signal from Nanette they all rose and moved off to other parts of the room, leaving her alone, glaring up at him.

"How did you get in here, you despicable little worm?" She said, getting to her feet. "I will have the footman fired if he accepted your gold. That is something I will never do. You are nothing but a silly little boy. Certainly not man enough for the charms of a woman like me. The richest, most handsome men in San Francisco flock to me each evening, like bees to honey. And you think I would have any time for you? No *Monsieur*, I have no time for you and I never will. You had your one and only chance with me—which you never deserved—and acted like a young pup. No more! Go away! I never want to see you again! And if I do I will ask one of my gentlemen friends to visit you with his bowie knife."

"Didn't expect to see you here today," Pádraig shouted to Diego the next morning over the noise of the crowd gathered on the wharf waiting to board the coastal steamship. "Come down to see the new side wheeler did ya?"

"I'm leaving San Francisco, Pádraig." Diego pushed his way to his friend's side.

"Leavin'? Leavin' San Francisco are ya?"

"I've seen what I wanted to see, Pádraig. I'm not much of a city boy."

"Wished we'd gotten better acquainted. Take care while yer travelling."

"Don't worry, I will." Diego patted his hand on the waistband of his trousers grinning at Pádraig. "Gonna keep my gold on me the whole time in this new money belt, like you suggested."

Diego shook Pádraig's hand and followed the rest of the crowd queuing up to board the steamship *Yankee*.

As the ship left the wharf and made its way past the flotilla of abandoned sailing ships just outside the cove, Diego's hand went to his waist where his fingers traced the outline of his money belt under his trousers. He had enough, he told himself, enough for a good life in Santa Barbara. He would surely have spent it if he stayed in San Francisco. His mother would be pleased that he was returning to help run the rancho. Angry, too. She would be very angry with him for staying away so long without letting her know he was all right. He wondered what Victoriano had told her when the vaqueros returned from Stockton. Her anger would fade quickly when he was safely back home with a belt full of nuggets. He could only imagine the things she could do with that much gold.

Yankee picked up speed as she reached the open waters of the Bay. He felt the vibration under his feet and heard the *wa-rump, wa-rump, wa-rump* pounding of the steam-driven pistons beneath him. Going to the rail, he peered down over the side. The big wheel was turning faster, the paddles digging deeper into the dark water with a cresting and falling *woosh, woosh, wooshing* sound. More quickly than he could have imagined, the village of San Francisco, hard pressed against the beach and hemmed in by the sand hills to the west, vanished from view as they passed Goat Hill and turned toward the Golden Gate. All the tents and wooden buildings, all the smells of ripe garbage and offal, all the men moving back and forth along the mudded streets, calling out in a dozen different languages, faded then disappeared. He didn't belong there, he told himself one more time. His relief at leaving was palpable.

Even though a clear sky bathed the bay in strong sunlight, dense fog still shrouded the Golden Gate, as if a curtain of gray gauze separated the fantasy that was San Francisco from the outside world, like a stage curtained off from the audience. The world of his mother's rancho down the coast was the real world, he told himself. A world of cattle and horses, high mountains and oak-studded valleys, vaqueros and rancheros, and no harlots like Nanette. The searing pain of her rejection came over him once again as he thought of her.

Yankee pierced the fog searching for open water. The *wa-rump, wa-rumping* of the pistons and the *wooshing* of the paddles were the only sounds now. Moisture formed little drops on Diego's cheeks and in his hair. After a few more minutes he left the rail and entered the ship's main salon. The large room, handsomely appointed with white furniture and gilt edged woodwork, was deserted, save for the ship's captain sitting alone at a table near the bar.

Diego approached him. "Will we be slowed much by this fog?"

"Slowed? By God not slowed at all. We have a schedule to keep and I'm bound to better it. *Yankee's* new to these waters, and I aim to set a record with her this run. She's one of the finest steamers ever built. Equal to any other in point of speed. She's as strong as wood, iron and copper can make her. She will be well known and praised by the Californians. Full speed ahead, I say. I'm Henry Osborne, captain of this vessel, and I'm bound to make a name for myself. Will you sit and take a drink with me, young man?"

Diego thanked the captain for his offer but declined, telling him he still had to find his berth and settle in.

"You'll sleep like a newborn tonight, I promise you that," Captain Osborne told him as Diego moved away.

In fact, Diego had a restless sleep that night. The snoring of a dozen other men in the cabin, combined with the incessant pounding of the steam engine pistons, and the awkward feel of the money belt pressing on his stomach, kept him awake through the dark hours.

By morning the distant outline of Monterey was reassuring. But toward evening fog returned. The ship steamed southward again into its private world of gray. After dinner, as he passed through the salon on his way back to his berth, Diego encountered the captain again. "Damn fog!" He said. "We'll round Point Conception in a few hours and have to feel our way through the channel to Santa Barbara. Pretty narrow there, you know. But don't you worry, son, we'll land you there safe and sound in the morning. First sea voyage for you, is it? Thought so."

"My father captained a ship on these coastal waters years back, but he never took me with him. His was a sailing ship. He told me tales of the fog. Lost a man overboard one time, he said."

"Times were different back then. Safer now."

Diego sat with the captain for a while, then said good night and headed for his berth. He slipped in and out of another light sleep, trying to picture his reunion with his mother. Hours later he was shaken awake. He heard men in the bunks around him crying out as they were thrown on the cabin floor. The ship shuddered with a grinding, cracking sound and stopped moving. Timbers in the hull groaned. The ship rocked gently back and forth like a cork on a millpond for a few seconds longer, and finally settled motionless.

"What's happened?" One of the half-asleep men called out.

No one answered.

In the darkness he saw the outlines of men crawling around on hands and knees, trying to pull themselves upright, but the cabin floor was tilted at an alarming angle.

The stranger in the bunk next to his, an American, got to his feet. "We're aground," he said with an authoritative tone in his voice. "We're not moving because the ship's run aground, probably on some rocks."

"We may sink," another man shouted. "We've got to get out of here."

"Come along with me," the American said to Diego. "No need to panic. Not yet anyway. Let's get out on deck and see what's going on." He started across the cabin floor toward the door as if he were climbing a steep hill. When he pulled on the handle the door flew open inward, almost flinging him across the cabin.

Sounds of waves breaking against the ship's hull were a constant backdrop to the shouts and screams of the passengers pushing their way onto the main deck.

"Stay with me. You look scared. Don't let the others panic you." The American tried to steer Diego with a firm hand on his shoulder.

"We're on the rocks." An officer came along the deck from the wheelhouse and called out to the frightened passengers. "We're not far offshore. Musta hit a reef not on the charts. Damn poor charts, I'd say."

"Are we to drown?" a woman screamed.

"Please stay calm, Madam."

"What are we to do?" the man next to her shouted at the officer.

Before he could answer the steamer slipped farther off the rocks, listing at a more precarious angle. The lee rail sank perilously closer to the water. New screams drowned out whatever instructions the officer was trying to give them.

"Ship's gonna sink," a voice hollered from farther down the deck. "Must have a huge gash in her side. Wooden hull, ya know."

"We can't stay on the ship," the American told Diego. "No way they can launch lifeboats at this angle. We'll have to say a prayer and swim for it. Pray the beach is not far off. You can swim, can't you?"

Diego wasn't a good swimmer and didn't know how far he could swim in the ocean at night. "Stay with me, please," he said.

They pushed their way through the throng of panicked people to the rear of the ship. Finding space at the rail, the older man, Diego made him out to be in his forties, peered over the side, then pointed. "There's clear water here, no rocks I can see. The coast will be in that direction."

"Are you sure?"

"No, I'm not. Fog's too thick to see anything. A lot of these folks may well drown when the ship rolls off the rocks and sinks. I'll stay with you if we jump."

Diego still held back. The American seemed certain, but Diego didn't understand why the man was staying with him. On the other hand, he didn't want to be left alone. Going along was easiest.

The man grabbed him by the arm and pulled him to the rail. "You will surely perish if you stay here," he said over the sound of waves breaking against the rocks. "Climb over the rail. Jump as far out as you can."

Diego did. He hit the water like a stone and couldn't stop sinking. He touched bottom and pushed off, fighting to regain the surface. He gulped for air, but was pulled down again before he could swim. Again he pushed off, but this time he barely rose. He struggled for the surface. But he couldn't reach it. Fear engulfed him as he sank down again. He fought against whatever was holding him down, but it was impossible to get back to the surface. He needed air. His lungs felt they would explode. The pounding sound in his ears was a drum beating louder and louder. The water that held him prisoner was black, he had no sense of which way was up. His disorientation made his panic overwhelming. No longer sure where the surface was he thought he was about to drown. The cold, black waters embraced him, coaxing him to stop fighting. He began to give in to the feeling. Then something tugged at his waist. He felt a pair of hands. Suddenly he was buoyant again and rising toward the surface. When he got there he gasped for breath. His lungs burned.

"Swim!" the older man urged as Diego bobbed on the surface, fighting to regain air in his lungs. "You'll be okay. It was unhitch your belt or let you drown."

<hr>

The shrill cawing of gulls awakened Diego. The smell of decomposing seaweed confused him at first until he opened his eyes. He saw he was on the apron of a beach several hundred feet from the water. The fog was gone, lying far off shore in a thick leaden band, and the rising sun colored the scattered high clouds in hues of pewter and pink and orange. Like some monster risen from the depths, the steamship *Yankee* glared at him. It still perched on the rocks fifty yards offshore, tilted at a macabre angle, but holding fast. Waves breaking around her sounded like distant gunshots.

As he rubbed his eyes fully awake he saw people moving about, holding on to the rail or inching cautiously along the decks. He reached down to touch the gold secure in his belt. A sound escaped his throat, more whimper than anything else. Gone! Sunk in deep water. The events of last night came flooding back in nightmare vividness. Looking around the beach he saw the American man snoring loudly farther back from the water at the base of a twenty-foot-high bluff. He got to his feet and walked over to him. He glared down for a few seconds, then dropped to his knees and shook the man roughly.

"Look!" He shouted in the man's ear, "Look out there! All the people are safe on the steamer. I've lost all my gold because of you. I almost drowned for no reason."

The American awoke abruptly. He stared out at the steamer. "So it is. Sorry, I thought we were goners if we stayed aboard."

"I lost all my gold. All of it was in the belt!"

"Sorry, lad, I said that. I did save your life you know."

"Did you lose your gold?"

"Oh, no, I don't have any gold." He reached into a pocket of his still wet jacket. "Guess all my cigars are ruined though."

"What am I to do now? I was taking it to my mother."

"I suppose you could swim out and dive for it. I hope you're not blaming me. I thought the ship would surely sink. Thought everyone would drown when it did. I was trying to save you."

Diego groaned. "I'll never find it."

"Don't you want to try?"

"I'm not a good swimmer. You saw that."

"Your choice is to dive for the belt or stop fretting over it."

Diego got slowly to his feet. He walked to the water's edge, looking out toward the rock ledge that held *Yankee*. It was a benign morning. The few clouds in the sky gave up their glow as the low sun climbed higher above them. The water lapped against the rocks, but farther out white-tipped waves signaled a rising wind from the west. He stood fixed to the spot for several minutes before he walked into the water and stopped when it reached his waist.

Feeling despair deeper than he'd ever known before in his life, Diego turned his back on the ocean. His gold seemed so close, but he knew he had lost it forever. Coming back onto the beach, his loss chewed at him the way a raccoon in Angels Camp had chewed at a leg trying to free itself from a trap.

"If you're not going back out there we should get on with finding out where we are."

"I can't do it," he moaned.

"Come now, you've a long life ahead, young man," the American said, trying to assuage Diego's agony. "What's done is done. If you're not going to dive for the belt it's time we moved on."

Diego took one last look at the rocks that held *Yankee* captive, feeling the dullness in his mind that hopelessness brings. Then he looked away from the water. Above the beach he saw a flat, narrow plain stretching toward low foothills that rose into three- and four thousand-foot peaks where early morning sun glinted off golden sandstone outcroppings. The slopes were covered with ceanothus and Manzanita trees.

"I know where we are. Probably no more than ten or fifteen miles from our rancho. There's a trail."

"Splendid. We can walk there."

"We?"

"Well, I've got to get back to civilization, don't I? It's a start. How far to Santa Barbara from your rancho?"

"Another fifteen miles."

"Let's get started then. Name's King, by the way, Preston King."

"Diego Austen."

"Good to make your acquaintance Diego Austen. And sorry I am about your gold. If you don't want to take a swim for it we should get going so we can be at your rancho by dark."

Diego stared at Preston King and thought dark, angry thoughts, but kept his mouth shut. He turned around once more to look at the stranded steamship and the water that hid his gold. For a moment he reconsidered. Then, desolate, and feeling an ache deep in his stomach, he turned away and climbed off the beach.

Walking east along the wheel-rutted trail, they saw no signs of life save for cattle grazing on bunch grass on the narrow plain, spotted with live oak and sycamore trees.

"This is a fair land. Plenty of water?" King asked as they walked along. The sun was higher in the eastern sky now, creating pinpoints of dazzling light on the ocean water on their right.

"Most years. Streams run out of the mountains with plenty of water all year when there's enough rain during the winter."

They walked on several miles, with King taking in the details of everything he saw and asking questions as they went. The morning air was still cool, but the day was getting warmer. They stopped at a narrow stream crossing so King could kneel down and cup his hands to drink the clear water.

Diego stood to one side, looking at him as he drank. "Why did you come here?" He asked.

"No real reason. I wanted to see the ranch land. It's wonderful land—mountains and ocean, and grazing land in between. I'd own some if I could."

"Live here you mean? Rancheros own all this land. It's not like in the north. Nothing for sale here. Why would you want land here anyway?"

"To live comfortably. Cattle raising could be profitable. Only a dream though, I don't have the gold to buy land. It is a fair land though, along the coast, isn't it? Land's always the best investment you can make, ya know."

Diego shrugged indifference and waded across the stream. "Not for Yankees," he muttered under his breath.

"What's that you said?"

"Nothing."

It was late afternoon, with long shadows preceding them, when Diego recognized the familiar terrain of Cañada del Corral. A smile brightened his face as the outline of the tall mountains to the north became familiar, and the oak trees that grew in the shallow valleys seemed like remembered old friends. The Santa Barbara Channel's waters stretched lazily to the south, a shimmering carpet of white-tipped azure all the way to Santa Rosa Island. In that moment Diego realized just how much he had missed his home, missed his mother. The picture of her grew in his mind's eye as he quickened his steps—a trim woman, always young, with a beautiful face and turquoise blue eyes that lit up when she smiled. The joy of returning home was leavened by the gnawing awareness of his disrespect of her. He had left his mother and dishonored the memory of his father, and now he was returning home with nothing to show for two years of his life.

"What's all that going on over there?" King's question roused Diego from his melancholy.

He looked where King pointed. There was a cluster of shabby huts and tents on the hillside just off the trail leading down into the canyon where the hacienda was hidden from view.

"Those your people?"

"Don't know who they are. Not our vaqueros." The sight of several open fires with men and women squatting around them made Diego anxious.

Rounding the last bend in the trail, he saw the hacienda in twilight. His mother stood in the courtyard talking with one of the vaqueros he thought might be Timeteo. His young brother, Jerome, stood at her side, taller and older than he remembered. Delfina looked older too, a little thicker in the middle, but still beautiful. He broke into a run, leaving Preston King behind.

"Mama," he shouted rushing to embrace her.

Delfina dropped Jerome's hand and took a step away from the vaquero. She stood alone, as if frozen in place, silent, her face a blank mask.

"I am home." He wrapped his arms around her, feeling the comfort of her body against him, but she felt limp in his arms.

"I thought you were dead," she said in a dull voice.

"I'm home to stay. I was at the diggings."

She seemed in shock. But as she grasped the reality of his return her eyes grew intensely bright. "How could you?" She had resentment in her voice that stabbed at him. "How could you not send word to me? What was I supposed to think? The vaqueros said you disappeared just before they started back. How could you be so cruel to me?"

"I am sorry, Mama," was all he could manage. His shame welled up, blurring his eyes, creating an aching lump in his chest. He was crestfallen she was angry, not joyous at his return. Tears ran down his cheeks.

"I am sorry, Mama," he said again in a humble tone. "I must apologize to Victoriano, too."

"Victoriano is dead. Murdered by a bandit coming back after

the drive. He was..."

"Did he have all the gold from the sale of the cattle? Are we poor again, Mama?" The ache in his chest grew.

"Victoriano was very smart," Timeteo, the vaquero standing off to the side of Delfina, broke in. "He divided the gold among us. We escaped with most of it."

"I lost all my gold, mama."

She looked at him, sadness dimming her eyes.

"Your son almost drowned. We were shipwrecked." Preston King had come into the courtyard by now and stood well back from the others. "If he hadn't let go of his money belt it would have dragged him under, drowned him as he tried to swim ashore."

"Who are you?"

"Preston King at your service, Madam."

Delfina and Preston King inspected each other over the distance separating them. Her look was guarded and questioning, but King was plainly admiring her.

"Our steamer ran onto the rocks. We both lost everything but the clothes we wear."

"I am sorry for you, Señor King. You are welcome to stay with us overnight. Longer if need be. Did you lose your gold, too?"

"No Madam, I didn't. I had no gold. Your offer is very gracious, Señora. I would like to accept your hospitality for a day or two, perhaps borrow a horse to get to Santa Barbara. The beauty of the land I have seen as we walked along the coast impresses me greatly. I would enjoying seeing more of it before I return north."

"You are welcome to stay with us. I thank you for saving my son's life."

King smiled broadly at Delfina, a smile that seemed to match the way he looked at her.

"Who are those people camped on the hillside by the road?" Diego asked.

Timeteo stepped forward. "They are squatters, Diego."

"We are overrun with Americans trying to take our land," Delfina said, a desperate look on her face.

Diego acknowledged Timeteo for the first time. "You are mother's head man now?"

"Why do squatters try to take your land, Madam?" King asked.

Timeteo grinned at Diego. "*Sí*, I have looked after your mother since Victoriano..."

"The Americans have no respect for our land grants." Delfina interrupted, stepping in front of Timeteo and closer to King. "They say we have too much land and some of it should be theirs. Since there is no land to be bought they try to steal it by living free on it."

"We have tried to evict them, but they shoot at us when we get close. We don't know what to do."

"I'll go after them, Timeteo. I am not afraid."

"You will not, Diego. You seem just as headstrong as you were before you left me. You need to be cautious. Conditions are different now."

"I am not the boy I was when I left with the vaqueros, Mama. I am home now to help you manage the rancho. I do not like Yankees. The squatters will have to deal with me."

Preston King rose early the next morning in the cramped bunkhouse room he'd slept in. He dressed in the work clothes Timeteo had provided that fit well enough, with leather boots that pinched his toes, and went out to the corral to find the vaqueros already preparing their mounts for the day's work.

Delfina was there, too, moving among the horses hitched along the rails.

"Good morning, señor," she greeted him in English, not stopping as she approached each horse as if it were a close, old friend.

He stood outside the corral gate, inspecting the bustle of activity, but fixing his gaze on her. A fine looking woman, he thought, very beautiful, in the prime of her life.

Dressed in a long skirt, with dark riding pants underneath, and a coarse white blouse that covered her mature bosom, she moved easily from horse to horse, inspecting their condition. Lean, erect, with coal-black hair down to her shoulders and azure eyes that seemed to sparkle and flash like the ocean waters, she triggered strong impulses in him.

"Is it possible for me to borrow one of your fine horses today?"

"Of course." She called to Timeteo and pointed to a roan gelding she wanted saddled for King. "What are your plans, if I may ask?"

"I want to see more of this land along the coast. I was quite impressed by the possibilities I saw as Diego and I walked here yesterday."

"Possibilities?"

"There is so much empty land between the ocean and the mountains along the coast, I want to see more of it. It appears to be fine grazing land for cattle or sheep, possibly good for crop raising too. With so many people flocking to California these days I believe one could make a fair profit with the right crops."

"You would take up land here, señor?" She seemed puzzled and paused for a moment before continuing. "The land you call empty belongs to rancheros whose families settled here when the Spanish *soldados* and Franciscans first came to Santa Barbara.

The King of Spain granted Cañada del Corral to a soldado at the presidio seventy years ago. The others ranchos are much the same. These lands are our lives. I do not think you will find much land for sale."

"And yet American squatters are trying to wrest the land from you."

Delfina's face lost its nonjudgmental smile as she listened to King. It grew serious and soon wore a frown. "That is a problem, yes. I don't know what will happen with them. They have no rights."

Timeteo delivered the gelding to Delfina and mounted his horse just outside the gate with the other vaqueros, listening to the conversation. "I think it will come to fighting," he called out.

"It could," she agreed. "I pray it does not. I hope you would not do that, Señor King."

"I would not, Madam. But surely you must realize how the squatters see the situation. They see all this beautiful, fertile, empty land lying along the ocean and think it should be put to a better use. That's how Americans think. Most of them have no gold. Like me, they have been unsuccessful finding the riches in the streams up north they came to California for. Yet they long to make new lives for themselves here. What are they to do?"

Delfina handed King the gelding's reins. "You will have our hospitality as long as you choose to stay with us, Señor King. But we will never agree to give up our land or our way of life. I was brought to this rancho as an infant. I have raised my children and lost a husband here. I lost another man I loved deeply because I would not give up this canyon for him and he would not settle down on it. No, the American squatters should not expect us to give up our land willingly, without a fight."

King rode away from the corral and out of the canyon. Heading west, he retraced the path he and Diego had traveled the day before. In no hurry, he tried to light a soggy cigar and let the gelding lead him, but after a couple of futile puffs he threw the cigar away. He studied the open plains and canyon mouths he passed in great detail, seeing in his mind smoke rising from wood-framed cottages spotted on the hillsides. Occasionally, he saw small clusters of cattle, some just tiny images far back against the low hills, and some grazing in the shade of closer oak-studded meadows. He wasn't aware of just when the idea came to him. It was only a random thought at first. But as he rode on it seemed to grow, crowding out all his other thoughts. Without any conscious effort, he found himself on the beach where the steamer *Yankee* still rested precariously on the rocks not far offshore. The ship was empty of life now, already becoming an abandoned hulk, just a skeleton awaiting burial in the sand as the relentless waves beat against its wooden hull.

Dismounting, he hitched the horse to a tree at the back of the beach and pulled off the boots pinching his feet. He walked to the water's edge, enjoying the feel of the damp sand soothing his toes. He stared out at the derelict ship, replaying in the theater of his mind the events of two nights before. After several minutes of just staring, when he seemed welded to that spot on the shore, he stripped off all his clothes and waded into the water until he was chest deep. He swam toward the reef at the stern end of the ship. The water was calm, and clear, when he got to the spot where he remembered rescuing Diego. It took several dives, surfacing after each one, gasping for breath to restore his lungs to full capacity, before he saw what he was searching for. The money belt was wedged into a tight crevice of the outcropping that had grounded *Yankee*. Taking another breath he dove and reached for it. Startled by its weight, he let the belt slip out of his hand and sink to the bottom. He waited several minutes, catching several more breaths, until he was sure of his plan. Then he dove again, going deeper, all the way to the bottom, where the water was colder and darker, and a Garibaldi fish examined him closely. Securing a firm grip on the gold-heavy belt, he rose. Only the gulls overhead heard his exuberant shout of triumph when he surfaced. Then he made his cautious way into shallow water and walked out onto the beach, collapsing on the sand, his treasure at his side.

He lay there for more than an hour, letting the sun dry him, exalting at his success and daydreaming about the rest of his life. It had been a mediocre life until now, but a vast array of possibilities spread before him as he looked at the nuggets and gold dust in the palm of his hand.

Finally, he dressed and walked back to his horse browsing quietly on a clump of grass. He didn't mount and ride off immediately. Instead, Preston King scoured the area until he found a safe place to hide his money belt. Then he mounted and, smiling to himself, rode back to Delfina's rancho.

CHAPTER 8

1853

IT WAS SPRING of 1853, a full year since Parker's death and the successful opening of Hannah's pie cafe. As Hannah and Luc walked along the bank of the river, the full moon put a catch light in her eyes and seemed to brighten her face as she looked at him.

Luc stopped walking and turned to face her. "I am very fond of you. I hope you know that," he told her.

"I know, Luc. I am fond of you too."

"It's been such a short time that I've known you."

"Parker's been gone a year now."

"Is it too soon?"

"Too soon?"

"To ask for your hand."

She felt a chill and turned away, looking out over the river, shimmering in the moonlight. Frogs hidden on the banks croaked a raucous serenade as she searched for words. Then, in a rush, her words spilled out. "Please don't ask me that, Luc. Not now. Let's keep our friendship the way it is."

"I love you, Hannah."

"Don't say that. I am fond of you, perhaps more than fond, but I need time. I'm afraid I will wind up losing you."

"That doesn't make any sense."

"You could never understand."

She turned from him and ran off through the pines back to her cabin. Going directly into her room, she shut the door and collapsed on her bed, burying her face in a feather pillow to muffle the sounds of her sobbing.

Shortly, there was a quiet tapping on her door.

"Are you all right, Madame?"

"I am fine, Miette."

"May I enter?" Miette pushed the door open without waiting for an answer and stood in the doorway.

"What is it you want?"

"Only to make sure you are well, Madame. I heard your sobs and grew concerned."

Hannah pulled herself into a sitting position. She tried to smile at Miette as she wiped away her tears. "What would I do without you? You are the only one who cares about me."

"Not so, Madame. Monsieur Luc Benard cares for you. I know you were together this evening and now you are crying."

"How do you know he cares for me?"

"It is obvious, Madame."

"He wants to marry me. I don't know what I should do."

"He is a fine man. A fine Frenchman. Better than any man I knew in Paris."

"I know. But I am afraid to marry him, Miette. I don't know what I want. I like Luc very much, but.... I'm afraid if I love him I'll lose him like all the other people in my life I've lost. "

A delicate smile brought the dimple to Miette's cheek. "You have enough gold now to have anything you want and yet you are confused. I have always known what I wanted, but it has always been beyond my reach."

"And what is that?"

"Children and a safe home. We are different, Madame, you and I. The most handsome man in Angels Camp loves you. Yet you refuse him. I would not."

"What should I do?"

"Perhaps you are a little crazy just now. Why not take some time to think? Maybe you should go away from Angels Camp for a few days. I will take care of the cafe and you can go to the City. Think about what you want. Luc Benard is too good a man to lose." With that Miette backed out of Hannah's room and closed the door.

When Hannah stepped off the steamer in San Francisco she was still unsure why she had agreed so readily to Miette's urging to come here. She made her way to the head of the wharf, where it joined Montgomery Street, and was immediately caught up in the tidal flow of men surging around her on the busy commercial street. She could see that the City had changed a lot since her arrival in 1850. Brick and stone buildings now rubbed shoulders with old canvas-sided wooden structures. Other, more solid, wood buildings were rising to three and four stories. But the smell of Montgomery Street hadn't changed. If anything it had grown worse. San Francisco had its very own unique perfume of rotting vegetation in the street, decaying piles of abandoned merchandise, spoiled foods of nations around the world, and accumulated human and animal wastes waiting for the next rainstorm to flush them into the bay.

Men hustling past tipped their tall silk hats and bid her good day. Talking in three or four different languages as they went by, they all seemed anxious to get on with their business. She followed them up Washington Street and turned on Dupont toward Pine, walking aimlessly, looking in the storefronts she passed.

Shopkeepers hawked their wares to her, but all the merchandise looked exactly the same. It seemed as if everyone was in business to supply the miners with everything they might need for success in the diggings, and a lot more they would never need.

In front of a small shop she stopped to stare at the window. Draped over the back of a chair, as if it had been laid out there by a lady's maid for her mistress, was the most beautiful ball gown she had ever laid her eyes on. Its long overskirt and short, puffed sleeves were of crimson silk delicately embroidered with intricate floral designs in white. The bodice, with a modestly cut neckline, and under apron, were gray-white silk, embroidered in similar patterns as the skirt, but with silver thread. She stood in front of the window picturing herself wearing the magnificent gown at a ball in Boston, surrounded by other beautifully gowned women and handsome men in formal attire.

"A lovely gown, isn't it?" a voice in the shop's doorway called to her, bringing Hannah back from her brief reverie. "My mother made it from a design a Spanish woman showed her."

"Absolutely exquisite," Hannah replied.

"Come inside if you'd like to examine it more closely."

She followed the young woman into the shop.

"Go ahead, you can touch it."

She took the soft silk between her thumb and forefinger, moving them slowly back and forth over the material, feeling its sheerness. Then she traced the outlines of the embroidered patterns with her fingertips. "It is a most wonderful gown," she told the shop girl.

"I'm pleased you like it. You have very good taste, Madam. My name is Sophie Laughten and I'm pleased to assist you. My mother made the dress. If you are interested in wearing it she can make the alterations so it will fit you perfectly."

"Oh, Lord, and wouldn't I be the belle of the ball? But where would I wear it in Angels Camp?"

"Did I hear a trace of the old sod in the lilt of your voice?" An older woman came from the back of the shop and greeted her.

Looking at the woman, she judged her to be Sophie's mother. "Perhaps just a wee trace. My mother came from Ireland when she was only a young child. I may have picked it up from her."

"Angels Camp, yer sayin'. I'm Emma, Sophie's ma. First time in San Francisco for you, is it? Your husband's a miner then?"

"My husband died a year ago. Caught a fever from standing in the freezing river too long. Couldn't breathe. His heart finally gave out."

"Sorry to hear, I am. So are you leaving California now and going back to wherever you came from?"

"I came from Boston, Missus Laughten, but no, I'm not leaving. After Parker—my husband—died I started a small pie shop for the miners in Angels Camp to support myself. I'm afraid I am rather stuck in California now."

"'Tis the same for my ma and me," Sophie joined the conversation. "My da died of the cholera in Panama. Never made it here. We're on our own, too."

"I heard you admiring the ball gown. Would you like to try it on?"

"I would, but there's no point. I have no place to wear it."

"No harm in putting it on is there? See how it feels. Sophie, go back with Missus Parker and help her into the gown. I'll go heat up a kettle and we can have a cupa tea together."

The gown felt just as magical against Hannah's skin as she imagined it would. Her reverie returned and she was floating around a ballroom in the arms of a handsomely dark, tall gentleman. Her gown swirled at her feet so just a brief glimpse of her ankles showed now and then.

"It's perfect against your fair skin and brown hair," Sophie complimented her. "And you've just the tiny waist for it, Missus

Parker. You surely would turn heads at the ball. Every man in San Francisco would want to dance with you."

"There's only one man in Angels Camp I'd dance with."

"You are a lovely sight." Emma came into the back of the shop carrying a tray with three teacups and teapot. "It's a good fit. Only a couple of alterations needed. You have a fine figure."

"It is a wonderful dress, Missus Laughten, but not for me, not now anyway."

"If it's a matter of cost we could..."

"No, it's not the cost. I have no occasion to wear a gown like this. Sometimes I wish I did, but I don't. I'd better change before I spill tea on it."

When Hannah had changed back into her day dress, she sat with Emma and Sophie at the small table in the cramped back room. They chatted easily for a while, then Sophie asked her, "Is it difficult for a widowed woman in Angels Camp? With all those miners?"

"Difficult? No, not difficult, just lonely. The men are very protective of me. They're all polite. Several—eleven by last count—have offered to marry me. So they can get their hands on my gold, I think. And for you here?"

Sophie and Emma exchanged looks without speaking. Hannah didn't know what message was sent, but it seemed to affirm the bond between them.

"I would say it is very hard for women of a certain kind—like mother and me—here in San Francisco. There are not many women here at all, and many of those who are, aren't women we are comfortable being around."

"What sort of women?"

"There are a lot of foreigners. A few are miners' wives, but the single women are generally of a lower sort."

Their Golden Dreams

"But surely a pretty, young, fair-haired girl like you would stand out from those others. Do you have a beau among all the young men?"

"Most of the men aren't good enough for my Sophie."

"Oh, Mother..."

"All these men want to do is gamble, drink and whore around. A good Catholic girl like my Sophie doesn't have much of a chance."

Sophie's face brightened. "The volunteer firemen are different. There are some nice young Irishmen in the firehouses... Pádraig's nice enough."

Hannah thought a moment. "I believe I met him once. I still owe him some gold from the first time I was here."

"My ma's right, though, most of the men are drawn to whisky and gambling," Sophie said. "They're not interested in anything else so there's no place to entertain a decent woman."

"We need more God-fearin' Christian men in San Francisco."

Hannah looked from mother to daughter. There was a sad look on Sophie's face and determination on Emma's. "You know, I think the same was true in Angels Camp because the men had no other choices. When Parker died and I had to earn a living, I served them wild berry pies. I didn't know if it would work or not, but once they tasted how good the pies were, they came in large numbers and paid me well. I think the pies reminded them of the good women they'd left at home. They still drink and gamble, but they have a choice now. And guess what? They've started cleaning themselves up before coming to my cafe. Their language is more civilized and they act like gentlemen—well, most of them most of the time."

"Your pie cafe in Angels Camp did that?"

"I hadn't thought about it until now, but, yes, I think it did."

"We have nothing like that here. Nothing in this big city. Fact is there aren't many places a decent woman can go to alone.

Something like that could be a place a girl like Sophie might meet a decent man. What do you think, lass?"

"Why don't you open a pie café here?" Sophie's excitement brought a glow to her cheeks. "It could be just the thing for a lot of men if they're looking for a reminder of their lives back home. I'd bet a lot of the volunteer firemen would come. And Pádraig."

Hannah laughed. "Imagine that. Me serving fruit pies to the firemen in San Francisco."

"Why not?"

"Is Pádraig your beau?"

"Sophie wishes he were."

"Oh, Mother, please don't start."

Hannah thought a moment and then laughed again, a smile broadening across her face. "Why not indeed. Maybe then I would have a place to wear your beautiful gown."

Luc was stunned by Hannah's rejection. Since Parker's death he'd spent so much time with her he thought she had feelings for him that were growing stronger. He resolved to convince her theirs would be a good marriage, but when he went to her cabin, Miette told him she had gone to San Francisco.

"To stay?"

"Who can say, *Monsieur*? I am here in charge of the cafe now. Perhaps she will stay away for a while. *Je ne sais pas.*"

The news sent him plunging into a deep depression. He lost interest in working with the other French miners on the river. He began roaming the hillsides around Angels Camp during the day, thinking about her, trying to decide what he should do. Hannah had stolen his heart. The images of her he saw in his mind as he walked haunted him. When she smiled her oval face came alive. That pretty face, with its full cheeks, slender nose and smallish mouth with fine teeth haunted his dreams and tugged at his heart. He longed to touch her smooth, chestnut hair again, and see the smile in her eyes so much he almost stumbled over branches and rocks as he walked aimlessly for hours on end.

Evenings found him downing a whisky or two at the saloon. Lost in his thoughts of her, he ignored the other miners packed in around him at the new, long, wooden bar. The men talked loudly, trying to be heard over the sounds of the piano, but he paid no attention.

"You the Frenchman I see all the time at the woman's pie shop, ain't ya?" The man next to him asked.

"I was."

"M'name's Hiram Blodgett. Don't see much of ya on the river these days."

Luc nodded. "Tired of the work, I guess."

"Made your strike have ya?" The younger man standing on the other side of Blodgett leaned over him and almost shouted.

Luc looked at him for several moments before answering. "Enough."

"Must be nice to make a strike. This here's my son-in-law Ike Parsons."

"Truth to tell," Luc replied a bit carelessly, "I didn't really come here to find gold."

Blodgett and Parsons both let their jaws drop.

"That so? Why'd you come here then, all the way from France?"

"To get away from the fighting. Best place I could think to come to."

"Well, I'll be..." Blodgett slammed his glass down on the bar. "Haven't I heard all now?"

"Run away from a fight, did ya?" Parsons pressed closer across Blodgett to look aggressively at Luc.

"Wasn't my fight."

"Wouldn't mind if you left some of that gold in the river for us if you don't want it. Me and the boy here are having a run of hard luck."

"Didn't say I didn't want it. Just said I don't need gold that much."

"What's the fightin' about in France?"

"French people don't want a king. Then, when they get rid of one, they think they want another one back. Every few years they fight over it."

"So ya just up and left France?"

Luc nodded again. "The fighting didn't matter much to my family. We live in a village northeast of Paris called Épernay. I was learning the wine and restaurant trade 'til the fighting dried it up. I wanted an adventure, so I came to the gold fields with a party of French miners."

"What will you do if you don't go back to the diggings?"

"Don't know. Been thinking that over."

"We all thought you was sweet on the pie lady."

A sad smile crossed Luc's face and faded. "Hannah Parker, you mean. She's a sweet young woman. I guess she doesn't have time for the likes of me. Been thinking about moving on, maybe see more of California before going home."

A few days later, Luc packed up all his belongings. Then he went to Hannah's cabin again in the faint hope she had returned. Miette greeted him.

"*Madame ne est pas revenu*," she told him. "I've had no word from her."

"*Se il vous plaît lui dire que je ai laissé, Miette.* Please tell her I have left Angels Camp when she returns. *Je suis venu dire au revoir.*"

"I would like you to stay, Luc. We could become good friends."

Luc shrugged and gave her a weak smile. "*Je suis désolé.*"

Miette's lashes fluttered. "I will miss you. *Vous allez me manquer.*"

CHAPTER 9

1853

LUC LEFT THE stagecoach he took from Angels Camp along the riverbank in Stockton and went straight to Fee's Livery and Feed Stable. He purchased the best horse and saddle available and set out north on the Sacramento road that skirted the swamps along the river. He'd given no thought to where he was going, only that he had to get away from the gold fields and try to get over the hurt of losing Hannah.

He rode to Sacramento and crossed the river, turning westward to follow it until an intense storm forced him to take shelter. The next day, under a few slate gray clouds that lingered, he guided his horse farther west, fording the Napa River and going north to Napa City, a shabby collection of wood and canvas shacks. That night, weary from horse and trail, he slept in a dilapidated hotel room he shared with two other men.

Early the next morning he continued north, riding through a pleasant valley hemmed in east and west by gentle hills that rose into low mountains. It struck him as similar to the valleys tucked between the low hills of the Champagne region outside his home.

Passing scattered cabins along the trail, he studied the fields behind them with a curious eye. Grains, some wheat, mostly barley, were the primary crops the settlers had planted. Alongside each cabin small vegetables gardens and flowers beds added spots of color. Milk cows penned near the cabins uttered low complaints as they tugged against halter ropes securing them.

Surprised by the sight of grapevines, he stopped his horse in front of one cabin and stared for several minutes. As he sat in the saddle, studying the vines fastened to wooden trellises set in the ground beside them, an older man straightened up from a woodpile where he had been splitting firewood with an axe.

"Mornin', traveler." The man set his axe down and started toward him. "Is there some reason why you're watching me?"

"Sorry, sir, it was not my intention to offend you. I saw your grapevines and stopped to admire them."

"You know about grapevines, do you?"

"I do, sir. My name is Luc Benard and I am from Épernay, France. Do you mind if I dismount to inspect them more closely?"

"Not at all. Luc Benard, is it? I can tell from the way you talk you are a foreigner. My Name is George Yount. Just passing through are you?"

"Don't know yet." Luc dismounted and walked toward the vines. Yount stayed close beside him. He was a man many years past middle age, with white hair that accentuated the roundness of his face. Not tall, Yount nevertheless had a sturdiness about him that belied his age.

"From the look of your vines they've been growing here for a number of years." Luc got down on one knee and took a handful of soil, looked at it, and held it up to his nose so he could smell it, then let it sift through his fingers.

"You know about grapes, don't you? When I came here in the 30s—was no one here then—I planted those vines shortly after I built the cabin. Got them from the mission over in Sonoma."

"They've done well."

"Just about anything you stick in the ground in this valley does well."

"Do you crush the grapes yourself?"

"Crush 'em? Hell no, I just eat 'em whole. They add a nice touch of sweetness after a meal."

Luc stood up and gave Yount a hard stare to make sure the old man wasn't pulling his leg. "You don't make wine from them then?"

"No, sir. These grapes are just for eating."

"Where I come from in France all the grapes we grow are crushed for champagne."

"Do tell. You grow grapes over there in France?"

"Not really. But when I was a young boy I was responsible for tending a small vineyard so I learned how to care for them."

"I'd be pleased to invite you in if'n you'd tell me about where you came from. Got a pot of coffee I can heat up."

It was obvious George Yount lived alone in the small cabin. Luc sat at a cluttered wooden table near the stove. Yount poured coffee into two almost clean mugs and joined him. He asked Luc to tell him again about grape growing in France, and continued to ask questions as the morning wore on.

"Didn't know there was so much to know about grapes," he said at one point.

"I grew up learning about grapes. Everyone in the part of France I lived in grows them now. Didn't used to, used to be sheep-rearing land."

They were interrupted by a loud voice outside the cabin. "You in there Yount? I know you are. Open the damn door!"

When Yount opened it, Luc looked out over his shoulder and saw a group of men on horseback, ten or fifteen strong, led by a rough-cut man in greasy buckskins. He had curly black hair and muttonchops down his cheeks merging into a gray-streaked beard.

"Whatya want, Kelsey?"

"You got an Indian in there, Yount? I mean to kill 'em if'n you do."

"Whatya do a thing like that for, you black-hearted sonofabitch?"

"Call me what you like, we'll never live peaceful in this valley until we've exterminated every last one of 'em. They're nothing but vermin. You got one in there? I think maybe you do."

"This to do about your brother, is it, Ben?"

"Damn right!"

"Way I heard it he had it comin'."

"Damn you to Hell, Yount! No Indian's got any right killing a white man."

"You got no right, either. Army's going to settle the Clear Lake situation."

"I can't wait that long. Me and my men here are gonna kill any Wappo or Pomo we find, man, woman or child. Who's that behind ya? That a Wappo hiding in your house? We saw a dark man ride through town a while back. Send him out here if'n he's a Wappo and we'll finish him."

Luc stiffened. He backed up a step.

"He's a new friend and no Indian, Kelsey. You come anywhere near this cabin and I'll shoot every last man of you. And you know I kin do it."

Kelsey looked around from his saddle. "We mean you no harm, Yount, so we'll ride on. But if I hear you're hiding Wappos or Pomos, I'll hunt 'em out and kill 'em straight away."

Ben Kelsey reined his horse around and led his men back to the main trail. Yount slammed the cabin door. "Damn fools. When I was trapping beaver in the Rockies I had 'nough trouble with Indians without looking for it."

"What's got him so angry?"

"Hard to tell what happened. Some Pomo at Clear Lake killed his brother and another man. Likely they deserved it. They was ranching there and didn't treat the Indians working for 'em very well. Ben and some others found their bodies and there's been hell to pay around here ever since."

Luc went quiet. Looking around the sparsely furnished cabin, he noticed for the first time the rifle niches in the chinks of the log walls. "Seems as if all the Yankees in California are rotten-mean."

"Not all, but most of the new ones is—the gold brung 'em. They do what they please and don't worry themselves over who gets in their way."

"Kelsey thought I was an Indian. I saw the way he looked at me."

"Not all of us are like the Kelseys, but the men coming overland from the states now think California's the land of milk and honey like the Good Book says. They think God gave 'em California to do with what they pleased. You afraid?"

"No, sir, I'm not. Fact is, I was thinking this beautiful valley might be a place to settle for a while. Grow some grapes of my own. You think there's any land as good as yours for sale?"

"Might be. Be pleased to call you my neighbor, too. Might teach me a thing or two about grapes. But you'll be on your guard most of the time watching for Kelsey and his gang."

While Luc Benard debated buying land in the Napa Valley on which to plant grapes, Pádraig Duggan was going about his daily activities.

"'Tis a fine day to be Irish in San Francisco, 'tis it not, Pádraig?"

"Fine indeed, David. No fires in the city and plenty of work for the lads on the wharves."

Pádraig Duggan and David Scannell, another Irishman from New York, walked away from the Independent One firehouse on Kearney Street, heading toward Portsmouth Plaza. It was an unusually bright day. The bay glistened a deep blue.

Scannell, a portly man ten years Pádraig's senior, with smooth, fair skin and a balding pate, had to hurry his steps to keep up.

"I tip my cap to ya lad. You've found work for our Bowery boys. They all look up to ya. How did ya do it?"

"Simple. Early in the morning I climb Goat Hill to look out toward Golden Gate to see how many ships will be coming into port. Then I hustle down to Independent One and the other fire companies, if need be, to line up the lads to work the wharves. Each of them gives me a small nugget or silver coin each week for organizing the work teams. If San Francisco wants a volunteer fire department, the volunteers have to make a living elsewhere, don't they?"

"I'm thinkin' a few more big fires like the last one and there will be a call for a full time fire department. Maybe a job for me."

"So you're headed for City Hall."

"Always good to show my face there. How about you?"

"Emma Laughten's shop. She's sewing a new dress uniform for me. Don't I want to look my best for the ladies at our next social?"

Arriving at Emma's shop, Pádraig paused for a moment in the doorway. Sophie stood with her back to him leaning over the worktable. He smiled. Pretty enough. She looked like all the girls he remembered as a youth in County Sligo—a pale, skinny waif, with flaxen hair and eyes the limpid blue-gray of Sligo Bay. He had to admit she had filled out nicely as she'd grown into womanhood.

"G'day to you, Sophie Laughten," he greeted her, entering the shop. "Is your ma about?"

"Aye, she is." Sophie turned from her work to offer him her best smile. "What has brought you out this fine morning? Come to call on me did you?"

"I've come to see about my uniform..."

"What is it about you volunteer firemen?" She interrupted before he finished talking, straightening up and giving him a scolding look. "More concerned with how you look than puttin' out fires you are."

"That's cruel, Sophie. The men of Independent One are always the first to a fire. But we want young ladies such as yourself to notice us."

"Notice you, is it? I've seen the way you look at some of the girls and it's more than noticing you want, I'm thinking. Most respectable girls I know stay clear of you Independent One boys."

Pádraig laughed, putting a sparkle in his eyes. "How is it, lass, you know about Independent One lads if respectable girls like you stay away?"

"Oh, Pádraig... Mother," she called out, "Pádraig Duggan is here about his silly uniform." She turned back to her work.

Emma Laughten came from the back room carrying a pair of trousers. "They're done, I think. Go in back and put them on and let me see ya."

Pádraig knew they would be perfect even before he put his first leg into the trousers. They fit snugly—the way firemen wanted them to fit. He started toward the front room to show Emma, but stopped short. A young woman with auburn hair that framed her pretty face was in an animated conversation with Emma and Sophie. She was holding a rumpled gown in her arms and her brown eyes flashed with the intensity of their conversation.

"...But *Madame*, you are the finest dressmaker in this city. I will have no one but you mend my gown."

"How'd it rip?" Sophie asked from across the room. "Some gentleman get too frisky with ya?"

Pádraig stepped into the room, but stood off to the side, listening. He was unable to take his eyes off the girl, thinking she might be the most beautiful he'd seen since leaving Sligo.

"Bonjour Monsieur. I am Nanette," the girl turned to greet him brightly. She engaged him with her eyes so he couldn't look away.

"Don't be wooed by her foreign-soundin' talk." Sophie took a step away from her worktable, holding a pair of scissors tight in her right hand. "She isn't a respectable girl, ya know? Just a plain trollop."

"Trollop am I? I'm no trollop, but you are just a common working girl." Nanette kept her eyes on Pádraig. "I do not think we have met. I would like to make your acquaintance."

"She'd like to relieve you of some of your hard-earned gold, is what she's meanin'. You might call her a workin' girl, too, working up at Pacific House."

Emma had stayed silent during this sharp-worded exchange. Now she came up closer to Nanette, purposely moving between her and Pádraig. "I won't be servin' the likes of you, miss, now will I? I've told you before, I do no sewing for your kind. You are a disgrace. I'll not work for Pacific House whores."

Pádraig's eyes jumped from one to the next, following the rapid conversation. Sophie stood with one hand on her hip, scissors still clutched in her other hand. Emma was more restrained, but her look was hard, warning the girl there was no room for compromise. Even with the two Laughten women focusing their wrath on her, Nanette held her angelic smile and continued addressing Pádraig.

"We are hostesses, sir. I am used to talk like this from plain-faced girls and their mothers. What can they do when they don't have the natural beauty I do? I pity them, really. Why don't you come with me, sir, so we may become better acquainted?"

For just a moment Pádraig considered the offer, but the look Emma gave him said he would never see his uniform completed if he went with the girl. "Sorry, miss, I cannot. I'm here to have my trousers fitted."

"Trousers fitted, is it?" Nanette gave Pádraig a wink, looking at his tight-fitting pants. "May I help?"

Sophie raised her scissors. Emma took a step closer. "Please leave now before I forget my Christian upbringing."

"Go!" Sophie commanded, menacing the girl. "Go, now, we are losing patience."

Nanette gave Pádraig a final, seductive smile and another wink. Then she went out the door still carrying her torn gown in her arms.

"A nice Irish lad like you has no business with the likes of that whore," Emma said. "You should find a nice Irish girl like my Sophie and settle down."

Sophie blushed. She gave her mother an embarrassed frown, but she quickly gave Pádraig her brightest smile of the morning, as if to send him a message as he left the shop.

The crowd poured into the firehouse, making so much noise Sean Doyle had to shout at Pádraig. "A grand parade, sure enough, and you out in front leading us. A fine day for Independent One, I'd say! We'll be having a fine party now for sure."

"Right you are." Aidan Coyne, an impish red-headed man chimed in. "The mayor did a fine thing honoring all the fire companies today, but didn't we lead the others all the way to City Hall?"

Pádraig stood tall, his shoulders back, beaming, his thumbs hooked in the waistband of his black trousers. The emblem Emma had embroidered—two crossed brass speaking trumpets in gold on a field of black—was across the front of his red flannel parade shirt. He glanced around at the growing crowd with a swell of pride.

He spotted David Scannell coming in the door.

"Look at your handsome uniform," Scannell greeted him. "You have done well for yourself. I hear talk of you wherever I go."

"Well enough, David."

"In truth, Pádraig, you are becoming a very popular young man in the City. A certain important gentleman has told me he would like to talk with you—he asked me to speak privately with you about a meeting."

Pádraig's face turned serious. "Important? Reputable man? Who might that be?"

"Highly placed in the City's Democratic Party he is. He knows you are popular with the town's working men."

"Democratic Party, you say." Pádraig barely let Scannell finish speaking. "I want nothing to do with Senator William Gwin and his southern Chivalry group. Nothing! There will be no slaves in California as long as workingmen have anything to say about it. Never."

"Pádraig, he is not a Chiv. This man doesn't approve of what Gwin and the other southerners stand for. He's a free-soiler. An Irishman, like us. That's why he wants to meet you."

"What does he want?"

"He knows the firemen and workers on the wharves look up to you. The Party needs support from those men in order to stand up to Gwin and his group."

"Can he be successful? I hear Gwin's got control of all city jobs and the party machinery. He's got his arms around everything."

"You're right. It would be a tough battle, but some Democrats are committed to changing the Party. This man wants to meet you to explain their ideas."

"I'll listen. Sure, I'll listen. I know there's a lot of talk about allowing slaves. If that happens it would put our Irish lads out of work, wouldn't it? Sure, David, I'll meet with him."

"He regularly comes to Pacific House in the evenings. I can set up a meeting there whenever you say."

"Give me a day or two to discuss this with some of the boys. Then I'll meet with him. Tell him next week, Wednesday evening." Pádraig stopped to look hard into Scannell's face. "Pacific House, you say?"

Pádraig told the footman at Pacific House his name and waited. Almost immediately a woman came to the door. She was lovely in her oriental dress that showed off the light brown skin of her face and arms.

"Good evening," she said in a soft voice that held a trace of the Islands. "Mister Scannell has been expecting you, Mister Duggan. I must say you are handsome beyond my expectations. I am Ipo, the proprietor here at Pacific House, happy to welcome you. Your first visit, I believe. I will take you to Mister Scannell now."

She guided him into the main parlor, where Scannell sat in a far corner. Almost instantly, a waiter appeared with a champagne bottle and two glasses on a silver tray. "This city runs on champagne," Scannell laughed. "You'll be drinking it from now on I'm guessing."

Shortly, the woman returned leading another man. "This is Lucius Macondray," she said in her soft, seductive voice. "If you will follow me, gentlemen, I have a private room where you can talk."

"A long way from the Bowery, ain't it, lad?" Scannell gave a deep, hoarse laugh that shook his belly fat as the three men followed her.

She led them to a small room at the rear of the building where plush leather chairs were set around a small marble-topped mahogany table. "There is chilled champagne on the sideboard, but call for the waiter if you want more or need food sent in." She smiled at each of the men and backed toward the door. Pádraig caught the faint whiff of her jasmine perfume as she left the room.

"I'm glad you agreed to meet with me," Lucius Macondray said when the door closed behind her. "Some of us have watched you for several months now, Duggan—may I call you Pádraig? That's an old country name, isn't it?"

"Sure, my men all call me Pádraig. I want to know just what you have in mind, Mister Macondray, so let's get down to business."

"You cut your teeth with the Dems on the Bowery back in New York, I'm told by Scannell here. That so?"

"'Tis. I was a young lad, just a runner for them."

"You've come a long way."

"Lucius and I have asked around," Scannell joined the conversation. "You've quite a following. Your men are very loyal."

"Not my men really, David. All I've done is put them to work. I've helped them and they've helped me. Simple as that."

"Precisely. We need men like you. Most of those boys are so thankful for the jobs you've found 'em they'd follow you to Hell if ya asked."

Pádraig got up from the table, feeling just a bit unsettled from all the praise. He retrieved the champagne bottle from the back counter. Refilling his glass, he offered the bottle to Macondray who passed it along to Scannell.

"The men in New York wanted nothing to do with slavery, I

can tell you that." He sat again and sipped his champagne.

"Agreed." Scannell said. "We've got different problems here."

"Why don't you tell me what all this is about, Macondray."

"First, this is all in confidence. We hope you will keep it that way—safer for all of us. My purpose is to offer you a proposition."

"It won't go any further."

"We would like to promote you for a city alderman's position."

"Me? I've no experience in politics. Why me?"

"Because you can win with party backing. And we need men in the Party who oppose Senator Gwin and his Chivs. You'll have no problem winning if your men support you."

"I see." Pádraig studied each man's face for any sign they were not being truthful with him. He caught Scannell's frown.

Scannell hesitated. He looked to Macondray then back at Pádraig. "I'm not a Chivalry man, you know that, Pádraig. But I must warn you this seems a risky proposition. In the end you might have to go up against Gwin and his men. You'd have no choice. They have the upper hand here. Indeed, they have the support of most of the recent newcomers to California—"

"That's because the South sees an opportunity here," Macondray interrupted. "They're encouraging men from the South to resettle here and vote for slavery. We have to stop them."

"Didn't we block slavery in the state constitution?"

"True enough, but that was three years ago. It was the only way California could gain statehood. And we had Frémont with us. A lot has changed since. Every steamer coming through the Golden Gate brings more southerners than Yankees—and not by accident. The South wants California. Our Party controls the city, and the city controls the vote in California, but unless the free-soilers among us get stronger, you might see slaves working the mines for their owners one day."

"We can't allow that!" Pádraig was on his feet again, pressing his hands hard on the table, leaning forward to engage Macondray and Scannell with the intensity of his look. "It would put men out of work. It would change California completely."

"At the very least it would split the state in two and I believe the southern half would support the South if it ever came to a test."

"War, you mean?"

"Sooner or later, I would think. The South will lose its power as more new states are carved out of the West north of the compromise line. By itself that could start a war."

"And if a war starts the South will need California gold," Scannell injected.

"Precisely. You can see how badly we need men like you to stand with us, Pádraig."

He had sat back down during the exchange. Now he leaned forward again, with his head in his hands, trying to see the possibilities the men around him were describing. "I do see," he said at last. "The Irish lads—no, all the working men who have come to San Francisco—will never support the Democratic Party if it supports slavery."

"Agreed. We need to start now to build support. That's why we need you to show them you are with us. We can assure you the alderman position will be lucrative for you. You can keep working at your other businesses at the same time. So what do you say? Are you with us?"

"Before I say 'yes' there are some things you must know. I've already said I will never support slavery in California. That means I won't publicly support Senator Gwin or any of the southern wing of the Party. I'll keep quiet for now, but if forced to I'll publicly speak out against him. Second, I will do nothing illegal if I am elected to public office. And third, I will never, never, do anything that would harm the workers of this city, especially the volunteer firemen. You must agree to all this if we are to work together."

Macondray and Scannell nodded. "It's agreed then."

The men rose and shook hands. Together, they went back down the hall to the parlor.

"Good evening. Gentlemen." A young woman, with curly hair the rich red-brown color of autumn maple leaves framing her face, approached their table. "Won't you please sit?"

Pádraig could not help noticing her slender legs and firm hips as she stood in front of them, and her partially exposed breasts that showed the ripeness of youth. She looked familiar.

"I know you, don't I?" she said, offering him a smile. "We've met before. You're a fireman, but tonight you look quite the prosperous man about the City. I am Nanette."

Pádraig returned the smile and nodded. "How could I forget a girl like you, Nanette?"

"Those women in the dress shop were mean to me." Nanette chose a chair across from the men where she could look at them and they could admire her. She sat with her legs crossed so that the slit in her gown revealed her thigh. "Such a handsome man you are, Pádraig."

Macondray and Scannell got to their feet. "I think we should leave you now Pádraig. We will be in touch." They made quick bows and an even quicker exit.

Nanette looked into Pádraig's face with a smile of anticipation. "You have some gold, no?"

When Pádraig nodded, her face broke into a broad smile that showed her full cheeks. "As I thought." She got to her feet and reached out to take his hand. "We won't talk of gold tonight. You will stay here with me."

CHAPTER 10

1853

THE FIRST THING Hannah asked Miette the evening she returned to Angels Camp after an absence of two weeks was whether Luc Benard had come by while she was away.

"Yes, Madame, he did. He came by once to see you, but went away when I told him you were not here. He came back again a few days later to say he was leaving Angels Camp."

In the stillness of the evening, sitting just outside the cabin, the women grew quiet. Only the chorus of tree frogs and the occasional screech of a raptor somewhere in the darkness interrupted their thoughts.

"Did he say when he would return?"

"No, Madame. He said he was not coming back. I asked him to stay."

For a moment Hannah looked out into the night. She couldn't find any words, couldn't even think very clearly. Then the moment passed. She willed her disappointment off her face and turned back to Miette. "I see. I am going to leave Angels Camp, too. I am going back to San Francisco to open a café there. Will you come with me?"

Miette gave Hannah a surprised look. Then her eyes took on a sparkle and her face became a dimpled smile. "Leave Angels Camp? *Mais Oui*. But who will serve the men here?"

"I came to Angels Camp because Parker was here. There is nothing for me now. We can go as soon as we are ready."

Word of their departure swept over the miners like an avalanche racing down a mountainside. Many were angry at being abandoned. Some pleaded with her to reconsider. Among the men making their way to her cabin were Hiram Blodgett and Ike Parsons.

Hiram stood in the doorway, his hat respectfully in his hand. Ike was behind him, shuffling his feet impatiently. "We've not come to criticize your decision, ma'am. Me and my son-in-law would like permission to take over your pie business," Hiram told her.

Hannah started to laugh, then stifled it as she realized Blodgett was serious. Standing at her side, Miette kept her stern look. "You mean you want to buy Madame's business?"

Hiram was taken aback. He didn't respond right away. Ike bristled. "Hell, we just figured when you pulled out we'd take over."

"What do you two know about baking fruit pies?"

"Well, now we don't know too much about that, Missus Parker, but we've been giving it a lot of thought. We figured with Concepción doing the baking we could learn the rest quick enough."

"We'd send back east for our women and they'd know what to do when they got here," Ike added.

"So you'd bring them out here to do all the work. Is that your plan?"

"Well, yes, that's about it."

"Ain't no other way we're likely to ever see our women again. Don't think me and Hiram will ever get out of this God-forsaken place."

"The men can be rowdy. They're polite enough to Miette and me, but they might not be so polite to you two."

"I've seen you in fights down at the saloon, Ike," Miette added.

"I win my fair share. I'd knock their blocks off if they got rowdy with me."

Hannah repressed another laugh and started to speak, but Miette interrupted her.

"You would have to pay something for the business Madame started, you know?"

"I suppose we could let them have it..."

"No, Madame," Miette interrupted Hannah again. "You have the cabin, all the tables and benches, the new oven, all the plates and utensils. All have value if they want to be in the wild berry pie business."

Hiram gave the two women a sheepish look. He twisted his hat in his hands. "Truth is me and Ike here don't have too much to pay you with. We haven't been as successful on the river as we'd hoped..."

"We's plum broke," Ike interrupted. "Tell it true, Hiram."

Hiram gave his son-in-law a sharp look that shut him up. "We was hoping we could work out some arrangement."

"Very well. Work something out with Miette. She is right, you'll have to agree to some kind of payment."

Hannah and Miette boarded the stagecoach bound for Stockton where the steamer would take them to San Francisco. Rolling down from the foothills they settled deep in their own thoughts as the coach careened around curves and bounced over ruts along the way.

"How old are you, Miette?" Hannah asked, breaking the silence.

Miette was startled by her voice. She straightened on the seat, stared at Hannah, but didn't speak right away. "I do not know my age, Madame. My maman and papa died without telling me. The nuns didn't know."

"I can't imagine your life in France."

"It was not pleasant. I'm here now with a better life ahead of me thanks to you."

"I remember watching you on our first stagecoach ride."

Miette blushed. "With those other women. We traveled together from camp to camp for safety, but we were never friends."

"When did you learn English?"

"When I came early in 1850 I had to learn the language quickly or I wouldn't have earned my keep. It was hard at first."

"I hope your life will be better in San Francisco. Have you thought about that?"

"In Paris tomorrow was always uncertain so I learned never to think too much about the future."

"Surely, you must have dreams. A husband and family?"

"I doubt if any man would have me. I try not to think of things I have no control over."

"Do you think I made a mistake with Luc?"

"You must look into your heart for a solution, Madame. Luc will make a fine husband for some woman. Many French women would favor him. Perhaps he was not intended for you—perhaps for someone else."

Hannah gave Miette a questioning look, but didn't ask. They lapsed back into their own thoughts as the stage continued down the trail along the Stanislaus River. The clatter of iron-rimmed wheels bumping over the rocks, occasionally causing sparks, settled into an almost steady cadence.

Arriving in San Francisco, they launched into a frenzy of activity. Ramon d'Bouviere, rich from his winnings at the faro tables, found them a three-story building on Sacramento Street, just north of Montgomery, a couple of blocks from the Merchant's Exchange. The price was high, but when Hannah calculated the money she would save by using the rooms on the second and third floors for their living quarters, she bought the building.

Next, she purchased all the furnishings and supplies for the cafe. But she balked at the price of fruit the local vendors wanted to charge her.

"What are we to do, Miette? In Angels Camp the berries were free for the picking. We can't make any profit buying them here"

Miette walked away deep in thought. When she came back to Hannah there was a sly grin on her face. "I think I have the answer. I will go back to Angels Camp and tell Hiram and Ike they must supply us with wild berries and other fruit as payment for our business. They can send Indians out to gather enough berries to send to us by steamer when they collect for their own cafe. I'll go back tomorrow."

One afternoon, as they were putting the finishing touches on the cafe, Sophie Laughten came by with Pádraig Duggan in tow.

"I brought my friend to see your new cafe," she told Hannah and Miette, giving them a clandestine wink.

Pádraig studied Hannah for several seconds. "We've met before."

Hannah continued to look at him. Then a smile of recognition crossed her face. "I remember. You helped me when I first came to San Francisco."

"I couldn't forget a fair young woman like yourself."

"I still owe you for taking such good care of me. I have gold now, wait while I get it."

Miette came to Pádraig's side. She offered him her hand and a welcoming smile that lit her whole face. "I am Miette, Hannah's partner."

Sophie took a step closer to Pádraig.

"Another pretty girl," he said, unashamedly looking Miette over. "The lads will surely flock to your cafe to see such lovely ladies."

Sophie stood close by his side. "Pádraig can spread the word among his friends."

"Do you think they'll come?"

Pádraig hesitated for a moment. "They will come for sure to see what you've got here. After that who can say?"

As promised, Pádraig brought young men to the shop that now proclaimed WILD BERRY PIES on a large painted sign over the door. Sophie and Emma brought their friends too. Other men wandered in off the street, curious about the cafe and the two attractive single women running it. Hannah and Miette bustled from table to table, greeting customers and serving fruit pies, grinning to each other over their new success. Over the next few weeks the men returned, sometimes bringing new friends along. Each day the number of pies Hannah and Miette served grew a little. Then it stopped growing. Hannah and Miette exchanged worried looks.

Diego reined his horse to a stop on a small hummock just off the main trail to Santa Barbara. Early light was bringing the landscape alive on a day not long after Wild Berry Pies opened in San Francisco. Sitting in the saddle he stared out at the land he loved. Above the foothills, the rock outcroppings of the high mountains reflected a brilliant golden glow. On the valley floor the leaves on the sycamore trees shone green and gold in the distance, while the coastal live oaks clustered in groves of dark, brooding green. In between, the canyons were flush with the blue blush of ceanothus and red-barked Manzanita.

But he wasn't alone—not completely—and that was the cause of his unsettled feeling. Why were those people living on land that would be his one day as if they owned it? They had no right, but there seemed no way to stop the tide of squatters from building cabins and butchering steers that roamed the canyon as if they owned them too.

He urged the mare into a trot down the path to block the approaching one-horse buggy so it could not pass. The driver was a middle-aged woman with a pudgy face and round body.

"You do not belong on this land," he called down to her from the saddle.

"Who says?" the woman shot back.

"I do. Diego Austen, my mother owns this rancho. You have no right to be living on it."

"I know who you are, but you can't stop us."

"What is your name, señora? So I can report you to the alcalde and sheriff in the pueblo."

The older woman looked at him and laughed. "Go ahead. I am Prudence Stillman. My husband and I plan to homestead the land back in the canyon. Your sheriff and mayor are Americans now. You know they won't stop us."

"You are breaking the law."

"This is United States land now. Our laws rule. There is nothing you can do. Mister Stillman will build me a fine home here." She slapped at the reins to get the horse moving, but Diego shifted the mare to continue blocking her path.

"Does your law say you can steal land from someone who owns it?"

"Our law says if land is left unoccupied a person's got the right to live on it, and if he improves it over time it becomes his. That's your law now, too. Mister Stillman and I will improve the land around our cabin. Soon it will be a fine home."

"Why don't you go north? There's land free for the taking there."

"Tried that. Didn't work out. We came from New Orleans and across Panama to get to the gold fields, but we didn't have much luck. So we came down here looking to settle and took a liking to this canyon land. We'll have a nice little home in a year or two. Now, I've got to get into that sleepy little village you call

Santa Barbara for supplies. We aren't broke, you know. So get out of my way and let me get on with it."

Diego watched the buggy disappear down the dusty main road. Then he pointed the mare up into the canyon, heading for a grassy pasture about a thousand feet above the valley floor where a small herd of yearlings had been put to graze for the summer season. Delfina had high hopes for these horses. A rancher on the Santa Clara River had offered a high price for them if they were trained for working cattle.

He climbed through stands of oaks and sycamores that dappled the trail with shade. The long, low branches of the live oaks reached out as he rode past, like the fingers of some monster intent on capturing him. Where the trail emerged into strong sunlight, Diego felt the heat, making him sweat under his sombrero and dampening the armpits of his shirt. He rode on in the silence of the upper canyon. The day had warmed sufficiently to free the turkey vultures from the high branches of the trees where they had spent the cool hours of darkness. Now they were taking flight again as the sun created thermal updrafts that sent them soaring in sweeping circles.

He paid little attention. This was his world, and while he relished the sights and sounds and embracing smells of the land as it heated up, his thoughts stayed with the round little woman who intended to take the land away from him. When he reached the pasture he was startled to find it empty. No horses came when he whistled, as they'd been trained to do. He scanned the pasture, trying to solve the puzzle of their whereabouts. He whistled again, but only a lone scrub jay swaying on a Manzanita branch answered him.

Near the edge of the pasture he saw hoof prints pointing farther up the trail so he urged the mare into a slow walk and followed them. The prints continued higher up the trail into the upper end of the canyon. There it joined a broader trail leading over the mountain ridge to the abandoned Franciscan mission in the valley on the other side. The yearlings' hoof prints were easy to follow to that junction, but there they became confused, as if the horses had begun milling around. Beyond that point he saw the herd's progress started forward again, increased by many more hoof prints.

When he spotted the ashes of a small fire just off the trail he knew what had happened. Indians! Probably Tulares from the Central Valley had stolen the yearlings. Combined at this point with other stolen horses from nearby ranchos they had been driven down into the valley beyond.

He reined his horse around and rode back to the main road along the ocean bluffs. Spurring the mare into a faster pace, he headed east to the rancho of Don Nicholas Bell about five miles away.

"Our yearlings in the high pasture have been stolen, Don Nicholas," he blurted out immediately on finding Bell in a small, makeshift office adjacent to his hacienda.

Bell looked up from the papers on his desk. "I know. Some of my horses were stolen too. Several nights ago. Other ranchos also lost horses."

"The Indians from the Tulare Lake?"

"Likely. Appears they came over the pass at Tejon and then along the Santa Clara River valley."

"What are we to do?"

At that moment a young woman slipped into the office. She was a year or two younger than Diego, but he remembered her from the days they played together at rodeos and fiestas growing up. The daughter of Nicholas Bell and his late Californio wife, she had the dark hair, brows and eyes of her mother. Her light complexion was her father's gift. The strikingly handsome girl reflected the best of each parent.

"Do you remember my daughter, Sarafina?" Bell said.

Diego turned to the girl. As he did, she smiled coyly then looked away.

"We use to play together, but I haven't seen you in a long time," he said.

"When Sarafina's mother died I sent her to school in Boston. She's just recently returned."

Diego gave Sarafina a quick nod then turned back to Bell. "What can we do to stop the raiding? Have you told the sheriff?"

"What good would that do? He has no way to enforce the law. He says it is up to the rancheros."

"We should go after the Indians."

"Perhaps. There's a cattlemen's meeting in Santa Barbara tonight to talk about forming a posse. We won't get our horses back, but we might kill some Tulares as a warning."

"My mother's loss will be very big. She was ready to start training. It will set her back a year."

"Her loss would be greater if you were killed in an Indian fight."

"But we must stop the raiding, Don Nicholas. Kill all the Indians in the Central Valley if we have to."

Diego said goodbye to Nicholas Bell. He smiled and tipped the brim of his sombrero to Sarafina as he went out the door. She followed him as far as the courtyard.

"I heard you came back from the north. I'm glad. Everything here has changed since I went back east, Diego. The old families don't socialize the way we used to. I'm lonely here on the ranch so I hope you might come back to visit with me sometime."

Diego was startled to find his mother sitting with Preston King in the sala when he got back to Cañada del Corral. She was visibly upset. King sat close beside her on the couch trying to comfort her. Diego went straight to her side and knelt.

"You've heard about the yearlings, then?"

Delfina gave him a vague, uncomprehending look. She had damp streaks down her cheeks from her tears.

"What about the yearlings?"

He realized he had misunderstood the situation he'd walked in on, but couldn't stop. "They are gone. Stolen by Indians."

"Gone?"

Preston King moved away from Delfina, straightening up on the couch as he did. "There is other bad news, Diego."

"You can tell him better than I can," Delfina told King.

"What are you talking about?"

"I have just told your mother William Gwin, the senator who represents California in Washington, has urged the Congress to establish a commission to test all Mexican land grants made before the war. To see if they are valid."

"Valid? What does that mean?"

"To test if the land is legally owned by the Californios living on it."

"That can't be! The treaty ending the war promised our land titles would be honored. We were all told that. The Americans signed the treaty."

"Well, it seems they have changed their minds," King said. "Everyone who received a land grant before the war must prove to the men on the commission in San Francisco that they have a right to their land."

Diego clenched his fist. "No Yankee will take Cañada del Corral away from us, Mama. It is rightfully ours. Not the government's. It was given by the King of Spain."

"Nevertheless, it's an inconvenience. If your mother is called, she will have to go to San Francisco. She should have an attorney to represent her and take documents or maps proving her ownership."

"Will you be our attorney Señor King?" Delfina asked.

He hesitated, but finally agreed. "If you want me to, Madam." His response seemed only half-hearted.

"Does this have to do with the squatters?"

"Maybe yes, maybe no, Diego. It's hard to say. I have heard that Senator Gwin's goal is to break up the large ranchos. He wants land available for Americans coming from the south. I've also heard talk that he wants black slaves brought to California."

"Never!"

"I don't approve of slavery as you know, but there is so much land here and so few people living on it... I have tried to buy land here but none of the rancheros are willing to divide their land. Nothing is for sale."

"We told you you would not find any."

"With no land for sale that's why there are squatters."

"The Stillman woman and her husband, you mean. When they push us off our land or force us to sell part of it, they'll bring Negros here to farm it, won't they?"

"Perhaps."

Suddenly Delfina's face dissolved in a torrent of tears. "That would be the end of us," she sobbed.

Diego busied himself around the corral and bunkhouse the next day. In mid-afternoon, when he looked up he saw Sarafina Bell riding down the path toward the corral. Dismounting, she came to stand by the fence across from him. She was young, slim, graceful, and pretty, he thought, grown up a lot since their childhood play together.

"My father sent me to tell you he has met with the other men whose horses were stolen. They say chasing after the Indians is useless."

Diego set down the pitchfork he had been mucking wet straw and manure with, and came to her side of the corral fence. "Don Nicholas sent you all the way out here to tell me that?"

She smiled at him. "Would you like to ride along the beach with me. I'm lonely on the ranch. My father is always busy. I thought... If you want me to leave I will."

"Wait while I saddle a horse. It would be nice to ride with you."

Together, they rode down onto the beach and then along the water's edge The strand was no more that 20 meters wide, with cliffs that rose above it, shutting it off from the land above. Shore birds and gulls were their only company, save for a wedge of pelicans that flew in a low formation just offshore searching for fish.

Dismounting after several miles, they sat together on a low hummock to talk.

"Are you glad to be back from Boston?" Diego asked her.

"Of course I'm happy to be home with my father again," Sarafina said. She looked at him with a shy smile. "Are you glad I'm back?"

He was surprised by her question. He thought for a moment, then told her, "I am glad."

"Would you like to spend more time with me? Could we ride together again?"

Diego couldn't identify the feeling he had, but it was pleasant. "I would like that. I remember how we used to play together when we were children."

"We are grown up now, Diego," she said. "We're not children any longer."

CHAPTER 11

1854

THE ENVELOPE GEORGE Yount delivered to Luc on his Napa land early in the new year had come from France. It was folded, scuffed, wrinkled and water spotted. The ink had faded almost to illegibility so the postmark of 1851 could barely be read.

"How'd it come to be in your hand, George?" Luc asked.

"Can you believe that envelope went by packet ship from France across the Atlantic to New York, then on steamship that took it to Panama where a pack mule carried it across the isthmus to a Pacific Mail Steamer that brought it to San Francisco?"

"A long journey. But you haven't told me how you came to have it."

"Damnedest thing. When it wasn't claimed at the San Francisco Post Office they tossed it into a dead letter bin. Folks go in all the time to sort through it, looking for mail. That's what I was doing when your name on the envelope jumped out at me. Can you believe it?"

Luc took the letter into the crude cabin he'd built. Sitting on a bench near the stove he opened it.

> Épernay
> 19 Septembre 1851
> Dear Son,
> By now you may know that we have a new emperor with

the same old name. No longer satisfied with being president of the Republic, Louis Napoleon has crowned himself Emperor Napoleon III. We French so despise kings that only being an Emperor would do for him. So far, affairs appear going in a good direction for France. No longer is there fighting in the streets. In fact, Napoleon's Prefect of the Seine, a man by the name of Baron Haussmann, has been instructed to modernize the capital and get rid of the narrow streets where barricades were built. Haussmann is laying out broad new boulevards and tearing down slums to make way for them without a thought to the peasants he is displacing. Apparently, they would rather find new living quarters outside of Paris than put up a fight.

We are enjoying our peace. Le Champagne is a happy region once again, more prosperous than when you left. The harvests have been good, especially the one now underway, and that is why I take up pen and paper to write you today. The market for sparkling wine is growing rapidly. Each day sees new vines planted on the hillsides around Épernay. We are using a new recipe that reduces the sweetness of the wine. We label the new champagne we make Brut because it is so dry.

We hear many stories about the gold in the streets of San Francisco. I do hope you have collected your share. And I hope the adventure you sought on leaving France has been satisfactory. But now it is time for you to come home to take up your place in the family business. The business grows ever larger and I manage it only with great difficulty. We all mourn for Claudine, but we cannot undo the sad events of the past. I need you here now, working with me.

I pray for your quick return to Épernay.
Your Loving Father
Achilles

Luc sat into the afternoon and early evening thinking about his father's words. They brought back a mixture of good and bad memories. The next morning he composed his response.

20 October 1854

Bonjour Papa,

I received your letter just yesterday. Can you imagine, more than three years after you wrote it? It is now almost five years since I said goodbye to you in Épernay. My adventure, as you call it, continues in California, but I have left the gold fields to try other activities, and it has taken this long for the letter to find me.

I accumulated a good stash of gold so please don't worry for my welfare.

I go to San Francisco occasionally, where your letter was found, but do not live there. I assure you the streets contain only the gold dust that has spilled from the pockets of foolish men. For the rest of us the work of wresting the metal from the rocks and rivers is tedious. Few succeed in acquiring significant quantities of gold. I have been more fortunate than most.

I have used a portion of the gold to buy a plot of land—about 20 hectares—in the valley called Napa, north of the Bay of San Francisco. It is fair land, much like the land around our home. Mountains hemming the valley are taller, but the gentle slopes west of my land remind me of Le Champagne. I have planted a few vines here and they do well, but the only variety comes from the abandoned Franciscan mission. The grapes they produce are inferior to our own and are barely drinkable, even when made into a harsh brandy called aguardiente.

I must tell you, Papa, that I am not yet ready to return home, but I do not want to abandon you in the business you wrote about. So here is what I propose:

You may have heard that San Francisco is a town very rich with gold these days and likely to continue that way well into the future. Men spend their wealth on all variety of pleasures and consume many bottles of poor quality champagne at every opportunity because it is the only champagne available. Most of what is drunk here is not up to the standards the good houses in Épernay produce. It is watery and overly sweet. So I think the champagne brut you describe would find favor here. If you were to send me one thousand bottles, I could sell them at a good price and build a reputation and regular business for you. In that same shipment I would ask that you include some carefully protected vine cuttings of Pinot Noir or Chardonnay grapes that I could graft to the vines I have planted. I think in a few years we could also have a good still wine business in California.

Do not be unhappy with me, Papa. I love you very deeply and do look forward to the day when we will be together again. I will let you know when I am ready to come home. Until then I will work as hard as I can to build our business for you here.

Your loving son.

Luc

To make sure his letter got on its way to Épernay as quickly as possible, Luc went to San Francisco a few days later and deposited it at the Merchant's Exchange, a three story brick building on Washington Street, where outgoing mail was collected in sacks for the next outbound steamer. Then he started for the City Hotel with an idea to taste the quality of champagne being served there. It was a bright fall afternoon with the sun strong, but not too warm, and a cooling breeze from the Bay. Walking west up Washington Street he reached Montgomery and spotted the hotel a block away. He paused to watch the bustle of men coming up the sidewalk from the direction of Sacramento Street and saw a young woman among them who looked familiar. She wore a woolen navy dress with a hem that swept the sidewalk, and a short jacket for warmth. She held a wide-brimmed hat with one hand against the breeze. Nearing him, she quickened her step. A smile spread across her face as she stopped in front of him showing the dimple on her cheek.

"*Bonjour*, Luc. How happy I am to see you again. I thought you had left me forever."

"*Bonjour*, Mademoiselle. I am pleased to see you, too. I thought you would still be in Angels Camp. What brings you to San Francisco?"

"I have left Angels Camp and live here now. And you, Monsieur? Are you living in the City now, too? How wonderful to see you again. I have missed you and thought about you often. Have you missed me?" There was a flash of intensity in her eyes as she continued to look into his face.

Luc squirmed a little before answering. "I miss many of my Angels Camp friends, but I have moved on. I now grow grapes in the Napa Valley." He paused to let her understand, then asked, "Have you left Hannah, then? Is she still selling berry pies to the miners?"

Miette's face clouded briefly. A touch of displeasure came into her voice, but she stayed standing close to him, renewing her sweet smile. "*Non*, Monsieur, we came together, to open a new cafe just down the block. There is a big sign with Wild Berry Pies painted in large letters. But, Monsieur, *il va mal*. It does not go well for Madame. Without the gold I lent her she would be impoverished."

"I can't believe that."

"*Oui, Monsieur, Il est vrai*. I would not lie."

"Take me to her, Miette."

"Perhaps we might go into the hotel for a refreshment and some conversation before we go?"

"I want to see her right now. Please take me to her."

"As you wish." A bit crestfallen, but taking his arm nevertheless, she led him back down the street to the corner. Along the way she gave confident smiles and greetings to some of the top-hatted men they passed. "I have met so many fine men in San Francisco, Monsieur, but none as nice as you." When he didn't respond, Miette pointed down the street. "She is there," she said in a matter-of-fact voice. "I must hurry about my errands now. I hope we will be able to talk again soon." With that she dropped his arm and turned back up Montgomery Street.

Luc paused in the cafe doorway. He saw Hannah inside, sitting at a table with her back to him, sorting papers. Her chestnut hair was wound in a chignon at the back of her head. Her shoulders hunched forward as if she might be tired. No one else was in the room, but he hesitated going in. He thought about the last time they had been together, wondering if he should have come at all. He watched a moment longer then took several steps inside.

"Hello, Hannah." He spoke in a soft voice hoping not to startle her.

Without turning to see who was behind her, she said, "We're closed."

"It's me, Luc Benard. I heard you had a cafe in town and came to say hello."

She turned her head to look at him. "My goodness, it is you." She rose from the chair, holding onto the back to steady herself. "I never thought I would see you again."

"Am I interrupting? I can come back."

"No, please stay."

For the first time since he'd entered the restaurant, he saw her smile. It was a weak, forced smile and her eyes looked dull and tired. Nevertheless, he cherished her face. They stood ten feet apart. Neither one took a step to close the distance. He felt as if he were standing on a hilltop looking at her across a deep valley.

"What brings you here?" She finally broke the silence.

"I saw your sign."

"So you are living in San Francisco now?"

"Oh...no." He realized he'd misunderstood her question. "I've bought some land in Napa. I just came down to make sure a letter to my father in France got on the next steamer."

"Oh."

The silence resumed. On the street the rumbling of horse-drawn wagons and the shouts of the men driving them were a steady background noise.

"And you? You left Angels Camp, too?"

She hesitated. "With Parker gone there was nothing to keep me there."

"But I see you've brought your pie cafe with you."

"Yes, I brought Miette with me too, to help."

"I saw Miette as I walked down from the Plaza. She told me."

"She wanted to come."

"You are doing well here then?" As he waited for her to reply he watched her features soften. A long breath escaped from her pursed lips, as if all the pressure trapped inside had been released. Her shoulders sagged.

"No." She said it in an abrupt tone. "Look around Luc. I am not doing well. No one is here."

As she said that she turned away from him. He went to her and put a hand on her shoulder hoping to comfort her. Turning at his touch, he saw tears glistening in her eyes.

"I don't know what to do." The tears flowed freely. "I thought it would be easy. It was easy in Angels Camp, the way you showed me, but here I don't have enough customers. The men come, but not like Angels Camp."

He nodded his head slowly, considering his response. "There are many more things for them to do here. Not like the diggings."

"I was a fool. I made so much gold from the miners."

"And here they have other places to spend it."

"I may not keep the cafe open much longer."

"Miette told me she was supporting the cafe with the gold she brought from Angels Camp."

Hannah's head jerked up, giving Luc a hard stare. "Miette told you that?" She waited for him to respond. When he didn't she gave a sardonic laugh. "She would say that. She sees only what she wants to see. I still have plenty of gold. I have been very generous with Miette so I suggested to her that if she truly wanted to be my partner she ought to have a stake in our success. Miette has her own way of seeing things. I am not broke. Miette is not supporting me, she has invested in the cafe."

He put his hands on both her shoulders and squeezed a little. "I believe you. I feel responsible for getting you into the wild berry pie business back in Angels Camp. Now I want to help you make a success in San Francisco. If you let me I will."

"After the way I ran from you, you would do that for me?"

"My feelings for you haven't changed."

Sitting across from Luc in the Wilson Exchange Hotel restaurant, Hannah thought about how much her life had changed since leaving Boston. She was a widow now, sipping champagne with a handsome Frenchman for whom she had strong feelings, in a high class San Francisco restaurant. She knew he had strong feelings for her, too. It had all been lost, she thought, but now it had come back so very fast. Her heart fluttered, watching him across the table.

She set the champagne glass down and selected another oyster from the silver tray on the table.

He raised his glass. "Here's to the life we've been given. I'm happy that I've found you again."

She touched the rim of her glass to his and smiled happily. A shiver of pleasure ran up her back.

Luc ordered salmon steaks for both of them and told the waiter to refill their glasses.

"Why did you think a pie cafe was the best choice for San Francisco?" He asked after the main course was served.

"I didn't think about it. I met two women here who told me there was no place where respectable women could socialize together with men. We thought the pie cafe would be a good way for men and women to meet."

"I suggested the pie shop in Angels Camp because the miners had so little to do and the ingredients were free. That's not the same here, is it?"

"I didn't make a very good decision, did I?"

"Look around and tell me what you see."

"Nothing special. I see a busy restaurant." She shrugged off the question.

"You are the only woman in the room tonight. Did you notice that?"

She put her fork down and gave him a quizzical look. "I don't understand what you are saying."

"San Francisco is a men's town, but it's not like the mining camps. No offense to your friends, but there are not a lot of respectable unmarried women here. More will surely come in time, and men will undoubtedly come because your pies are unique in the City for now, and delicious. But here there are other diversions your cafe must compete with."

Hannah thought about his words while she ate the remainder of her dinner. "So what am I to do?"

"Suppose your pies were the wonderful dessert at the end of a fine meal elegantly served in a romantic setting?"

She pondered a moment. "Like this place you mean?"

"Not like this. This is not elegant. This is a mediocre restaurant at best and there are many others like it in San Francisco. What I mean is that we could create a unique restaurant where the important men of the City could dine elegantly—privately if they so desired—and are willing to pay a hefty price for the opportunity."

"You think we could do something like that? How?"

"I was trained for this in Paris before the revolution broke out. Together we could create a wonderful restaurant."

"You never spoke of that in Angels Camp."

"It was not very important to me there."

"It would cost a lot of gold, wouldn't it?"

"It would take much gold. We would need to find investors to help finance us. But we would pay them back many times over I can assure you. I would like to be your first investor." He laughed heartily and took a moment to catch his breath. "Or would I be the second if Miette is the first? You already have the wonderful fruit pies no one else has. I can provide better champagne than anything being poured in the City. So already we have two unique products. We are well on our way to the finest restaurant in San Francisco. Of course we would have to change the name."

"To what?"

"I don't know. How about *Maison de Paris.*"

"I don't know, Luc." Her face drew serious with doubt. "It all sounds too good."

"Please think about it, Hannah. I am serious. You could become the richest woman in San Francisco."

She sat stunned at the table for the rest of their meal. Luc's ideas scared her, but the picture of them working together in an elegant restaurant captured her imagination.

They walked hand in hand back to the empty cafe in silence. Hannah felt as if she had been given a second chance with Luc. She trembled with a feeling of anticipation.

They stopped in the doorway and stood looking into each other's eyes for an awkward moment. He took a step closer to her. She didn't retreat. Rather she took a step that closed the space between then. Then he embraced her and she didn't resist. She felt his lips press softly on hers, intensifying the feelings she already had. She returned his kiss. Then she took his hand and led him through the darkened cafe and up the stairs to her room.

As she was drifting off to sleep, snuggled up against him, she heard a soft tapping on the bedroom door. Without an invitation it opened half way. For only a brief moment she saw Miette's silhouette.

"*Mon Dieu! Excusez-moi,*" the voice stammered. Then the door slammed shut.

Hannah laughed to herself and draped her arm over Luc's bare shoulder.

Finally summoned by the Land Commission to San Francisco to validate her claim to Cañada del Corral, Delfina waited outside the Land Commission hearing room with Diego for

Preston King to arrive. The room was on the third floor of a musty, non-descript building near City Hall. Its sole importance was that it had been made of brick so it had survived the most recent fire that raced through the district. She sat erect in a high back chair, dressed in one of her best silk dresses, the same azure color that matched her eyes, with a hat to match and a pair of gloves. Diego paced back and forth by the window that looked out toward the Bay.

"Señor King said he would meet us here." She tried to reassure Diego and herself.

"No sign of him." Diego was at the window for the fifth time in the last five minutes peering down at the street.

"I'm sure he'll be here. He told us he would."

The clerk of the Land Commission came into the foyer from the adjoining room. "It's time for your hearing to start, señora," he told her.

"Our attorney isn't here yet. We must wait for him."

"And who would that be?" the clerk asked glancing at his notes.

"Señor Preston King. He is coming from Santa Barbara to represent us. He is to meet us here."

The clerk gave Delfina a questioning look. "Mister King, you say? To represent you? I do not have his name on my list. Well, we can wait another few minutes, but then the Commissioners must get started. They have a full schedule today."

"A full day of stealing land," Diego mumbled.

The clerk disappeared back through the door to the hearing room.

"Please try to control yourself, Diego," Delfina cautioned. "We don't want to offend these men."

The octagonal wall clock in the anteroom ticked off the minutes that Delfina thought were speeding by. Preston King didn't appear. Eventually, the clerk opened the door and motioned to them. "We cannot wait any longer."

Delfina frowned. She looked at Diego and saw the anger deep in his eyes. "Señor King has disappointed us," she said.

"Deserted us, I think."

Rising from the chair, she followed the clerk into the hearing room, a wide, shallow room with a rough plank floor, empty, with the exception of a long mahogany table raised on a dais and a much smaller one with two chairs in front of it. The room gave the feeling it had been abandoned years ago and left to die, along with anything or anyone that remained in it. Three old men, looking barely alive themselves, sat staring at her from the high table.

"Good morning, Señora Austen." The man sitting in the center of the big table introduced himself as Thompson Campbell. He was slight and wrinkled, and carried a full head of hair, beard, and sideburns in the yellow-white color of advanced age. "We are here to validate your claim to the four leagues of land now called Cañada del Corral in Santa Barbara County. That is, if you can show us proof of your title. Please be seated."

Diego jumped in front of the men in a slightly menacing posture. "You have no right to do this. Articles VII and IX of the treaty ending the war in '48—the treaty of Guadalupe Hidalgo—guaranteed our right to the land. Guaranteed all Californios' rights. I know, I read the treaty."

"Please sit down, sir. We have every right. It was vested in this commission by an act of the U.S. Congress in 1851, and it supersedes the treaty to which you refer. Please restrain yourself so we can get on with the proceedings"

Keeping her face a blank, Delfina stared at the commissioners. They have no right to take my land away from me, she thought,

Diego is right. Then, in a soft voice she addressed them. "My right to that land comes from the King of Spain, not any Mexican governor. The king awarded the land to a soldado named Guillermo in exchange for the life Guillermo gave in the King's service. Josefa was Guillermo's wife."

Delfina seemed calm, sitting straight in the chair, focused on the commissioners, speaking clearly in English in a controlled voice. But the twisting of her gloves in her hands as she spoke betrayed her inward turmoil. Diego's face was unable to disguise his growing anger, and his fear of what might come. He couldn't put on a false face the way she could. She watched him struggle to stay quiet as the old man began asking her more questions. He drummed his fingers nervously on the table. At one point Commissioner Campbell had to pause in his questioning to ask him to stop.

"Señora Austen," Campbell asked, "was this Josefa your natural mother?"

"She raised me as my mother."

"Can you show us any documents written in Josefa's hand deeding the rancho to you after her death?"

"She wanted me to have Cañada del Corral as my own."

"Please, answer my question."

"None I know of."

They are going to take it away from me, she realized. The Americans are going to take everything away if they can.

Slamming his fist hard on the table, Diego rose again from his chair. He looked down at Delfina. Then he turned to the commissioners. "Damn you all to Hell," he shouted. "You are evil men doing the work of an evil government, intent on destroying our way of life. I will fight you until I have no breath left to fight with." He turned and left the hearing room, leaving Delfina siting alone at the small table.

When order was restored, Commissioner Campbell turned back to her. "Señora Austen, I have a copy of your baptismal record from the Presidio de Santa Barbara. Mister Preston King was kind enough to send it to us."

"Señor King?" Delfina was shocked. She tried to understand why he would have gotten her baptismal record from the mission and couldn't comprehend it. But there was a feeling at the pit of her stomach that began to stir.

"Yes, It shows that you are a child born out of wedlock between an Indian woman named Cayatu and the Spanish Comandante of that presidio named De Alba. The Guillermo and Josefa you speak of are not in the records as your parents."

"Señor King sent you these documents?"

"So are you the child of Josefa?"

She began to feel despair growing in her heart. "No, but you must understand Josefa wanted me to have the land. She and Cayatu, my real mother, raised me together."

"But there are no documents in Josefa's hand giving you that land are there?"

"She wanted me to have the rancho," Delfina said again. There were tears in her eyes as she spoke.

"But no documents."

She could only nod agreement.

"Then you are not the legal owner, señora. The Commission has no choice but to return the land to the public domain. I am sorry. We are adjourned."

CHAPTER 12

1855

DELFINA RODE OFF alone early one morning in the new year, shortly after returning from San Francisco. She guided her gelding to a tree-shaded meadow where white clouds with gray underbellies hung over the high mountains that were partially obscured behind ancient oaks. Dismounting, she let the horse graze on the tall bunch grasses and walked to a brooding old tree where she sat with her back against the trunk. A limb, fallen in some long forgotten wind storm, lay on the ground in front of her, weathered to crumbling tinder in the twenty-five years since the day she first met Will Thornton.

It was the same limb she and her favorite horse, *Reina del Mar*, had jumped all those years ago when she was just thirteen. She was showing off that afternoon for the handsome Yankee trader. *Reina* had soared easily over the branch, but then stepped into a gopher hole on landing, shattering her front leg.

"I am sorry," the handsome young American had said. "We can't save your horse. I have a rifle—I see you do not—let me end her suffering."

"No!" she had shouted at him, panic etched on her face.

"No choice. Your mare is in pain. See the look in her eyes. Let us do what we must for her."

"No!" Delfina was close to hysterical. She rushed back to the horse and lay down, covering the mare with her body and hugging her neck.

"Please... *Por favor.* Don't stand in the way."

She stared at him for only a moment. Then, getting to her feet, wiping tears from her cheeks, she walked toward him. When she got to his side she thrust her hand out and put it on the rifle's stock, her fingers overlapping his large hand. Looking directly into his eyes, she said, "*Reina es mi caballo.*"

She took the gun from him and went back to *Reina's* side. She looked down at the shattered leg, then turned to the mare's head. "*Reina hermosa, lo siento.*" She pulled the trigger.

With the exception of the decomposing branch, the meadow seemed unchanged in all that time. The oaks and sycamores were still the ageless grand old men of the land. Solons who kept their rich history private, they provided sustenance for the creatures who were the real denizens of the meadow. A golden-tailed squirrel sat on its hind legs at the base of another oak inspecting an acorn in its front paws before stuffing it into the pouch in its cheek. Red-capped woodpeckers tapped away in the upper branches, storing their treasures for a distant day, while white-bellied scrub jays foraged along the ground. In the upper branches a red-tailed hawk kept a silent vigil for unwary rodents and not far off she watched a young rattlesnake slither through the leaf litter in search of a warmer place to spend the morning.

This was her private world. Without Cañada del Corral she would wither and die, like the leaves of the sycamore trees. Nothing before had ever parted her from it. Will Thornton's quest for gold had been his life; Cañada del Corral had been hers. They had never been able to bridge that chasm. She had loved the land too dearly.

Remounting, she rode out of the canyon and down onto the beach. Josefa had always told her this cove, protected by points of land to east and west, was the real reason the appeal to the King of Spain had been made for a land grant. It was this place where her father, the *Comandante,* and the mission priest had conducted their smuggling activities, secretly bringing in shiploads of goods they traded for cowhides and sea otter fur, out of sight of passing ships. Josefa never loved Cañada del Corral the way she did, but it was unfair to blame Josefa for the loss. She had no one to blame but herself for the life she had lived.

She was slow to the awareness that the beach was no longer empty. Another rider came along the sand toward her. When she looked up she shuddered. It was Preston King coming closer.

He tipped his hat. "Good morning, Madam. I have been anxious to see you since your return from San Francisco."

"Anxious to see me? I hoped never to see you again. I have no words to describe you, you are an evil...."

"I would like to have a conversation with you," he interrupted her.

"You promised your help then turned against us. I have lost everything. Leave me alone now, you're despicable."

"I have come to tell you I have bought Cañada del Corral. I am the new owner."

"You? You swine! You evil swine!" She looked away from him, back into the foothills, out over the Channel, anywhere but at him. "So your victory over me is complete. You abused my hospitality then stole my rancho. Your wickedness has robbed me of my home. You are an evil and despicable man! Leave me alone!"

King leaned forward in the saddle and took off his hat. With his hand he wiped the perspiration from the band. His face was blank, with only a hint of warmth in his eyes.

"Surely you do not think I stole your rancho away from you, señora."

"That is exactly what I think you did."

"Then you are mistaken. I—"

"What should I think then? You own my rancho now. I have lost it because of the documents you gave the Land Commission."

"If you think you lost the rancho because of the records I sent them you are wrong. Those men would certainly have found them just as easily as I did. I spoke with several Californios in Santa Barbara. They all knew you were not Josefa's daughter. It was no secret I revealed. The old timers talked about the *Comandante* who was your father and the Indian woman he fornicated with. There are even whispers Josefa may have killed him. There are no secrets."

"I do not believe you." As she said it something in her head told her his words sounded true, like words she had heard before, so she stopped.

"You were going to lose Cañada del Corral," King said directly. "There was no way to save it. What I did was to make sure I was in a position to buy this beautiful canyon after the decision was made."

Letting the mare's reins go slack, she looked across the few feet of sand that separated their horses. She held her eyes steady on him and tried to guess his thoughts. "I will have to find a new place to live out my life," she said in an unsteady voice. "It may take some time."

"Maybe not."

She kept looking at him.

"I have a plan, if you will listen. Walk along the beach with me while I explain."

Reluctantly she dismounted. A small flock of shore birds pecking in the wet sand scattered as she walked to the water's edge. King hurried after her. "You didn't tether your horse."

"No need, he's trained."

"Just there's what I want to talk to you about. I really don't know very much about horses and cattle and I've just bought a rancho."

She looked at him with the first hint of dismay that turned into a sardonic smile. "You'll need to learn quickly."

"Yes, but it would be easier if you were there to teach me."

"Stay on the rancho that you own? I don't think that's such a good idea."

"Do think about it. And don't be too hasty. I know how much you love the land and I'm offering you this chance to stay. I certainly will need help."

She thought for a moment, moving away a few feet, looking out over the Channel toward the vague outline of the islands on the edge of the horizon, listening to the complaining sound of the wavelets coming and going over the pebbles on the shoreline. A V-shaped wedge of pelicans, flying west a few feet above the water, brought an involuntary grin. She was trying to weigh her love for all that Cañada del Corral meant to her against the sure knowledge King was trying to use her. She took in a deep breath that brought the smell of seaweed and salt with it, and came back at him with a biting tone.

"That would be a very difficult arrangement. You want me to manage your rancho until you know enough to take over? Then what? You send me off along with my horses and cattle? I don't think that will work."

King knelt down to pick up a small, flat rock. Taking his time, he inspected it, turning it over in his hand, feeling its ocean-polished smoothness with his fingers. Finally, he rose and skimmed it across the water. Then he looked around the beach before looking at her again. "You wouldn't have to leave."

"So you would have me become your head vaquero, then? Perhaps I would live in the bunkhouse with the other men? No, señor, I have no desire to work for you. I resent your arrogance in even suggesting it. I do not like you, Señor King. I would like to get as far from you as I can, as hard as it is for me. You know you must pay me for my stock. Then I will leave you to fail on your own, as you surely will."

"I don't intend for you to sleep in the bunkhouse." He ignored her insults. "And you would not be my head vaquero. You have misunderstood me, Madam. I am suggesting that I marry you, and you become my wife so we can manage the ranch together."

Shocked, staring at him utterly speechless, she felt a shiver crawl up her spine and sickness gnawing her stomach. How vile could this man be? She thought she had not heard him correctly, but she knew she had. Waiting until she had control of her anger, she blurted out, "Marry you? How could you think such a thing? You have stolen my land, my whole life, and now you want to own me, too. Get away from me, you evil man! You horribly evil man! You have done enough harm already."

He moved in close to her. She held her ground. A hard look came over his face and a new, more strident tone came into his voice. "You should think this over very carefully before insulting me further, Madam. My patience is limited. I am offering you a lifeline. Without it you are adrift on a very turbulent sea. If you accept my proposal you can assume your old life with only some minor adjustments. Yes, I will own the rancho. But you will still have your land, your horses, your cattle, your vaqueros. If you marry me you will have a father for your young son and the respectability you have not had since the Yankee trader sailed off leaving you pregnant. You are a half breed bastard daughter with a bastard son, not a good thing to be in California these days. I am offering you redemption, Madam. Think all this over carefully. I will not accept your answer now. I will come to the ranch in a week and ask again. I am very fond of you, despite your insults. I would be proud to have you as my wife. But I do have my limits. If you agree we could live pleasantly enough together. But be warned: if you turn me down I will throw you off this land that very same day. One week is all."

A week later Preston King returned. Delfina was expecting him. She told him to stay quiet while she ushered him into the parlor and pointed him to a seat. "I have considered your offer," she said, without any introduction, taking a chair across from him, "and find it reprehensible. But I will accept your proposal of marriage with two conditions."

"Conditions?"

"First you must provide a place on the rancho where my son, Jerome, and I can live separate lives away from you."

"And?"

"And you will sign a paper in front of witnesses."

"What am I to sign?"

"That upon your death this rancho, its land and everything on it will become mine or my heirs'."

Preston King smiled at her. "I agree," he said. "After I am gone."

CHAPTER 13

1855

THE OPENING OF *Maison de Paris* on a warm late summer evening was a major event.

"*Bonsoir*, Luc," Miette greeted him at the door. "You've created a bit of Paris right here in the City, no?"

"Perhaps just a bit, Miette. Enough, I hope, to please our guests. With your smile and pretty face, and greeting them in French, we'll surely put them in a good mood. Perhaps they will think they're in Paris."

"I am glad I am here with you, Monsieur." Miette beamed at Luc, holding his hand just a bit too long before releasing him into the main room to mingle with the invited guests who had already arrived.

He paused to look around, smiling his satisfaction. Spotting Hannah by the fireplace in the back of the room, he started toward her. She looked beautiful in the pale green silk gown with white embroidery Emma Laughten had made especially for tonight. His pulse beat faster as he crossed the room.

Well-wishers surrounded Hannah, but he still embraced her in front of them and kissed both her cheeks in the French style. "*Ma chérie*, you are very beautiful tonight," he whispered in a soft, private voice. "Your smile tells me how happy you are."

Hannah blushed. "I never could have imagined this evening without you, Luc. You've made all my dreams come to life, that's why I am so happy. The best people in San Francisco will be here tonight to see our new restaurant."

"And they will come back to dine when we are fully open."

She giggled girlishly. "Some privately in our second floor rooms. You were so smart to suggest that. How naughty!"

"I learned about *Cabinets Particuliers*, private rooms, in Paris."

"You must mingle with the others now." With a gloved hand she pushed him away playfully. "Everyone wants to meet the Frenchman who created this masterpiece."

Luc took a glass of champagne from a waiter's tray and began introducing himself to the guests. Hannah also excused herself from the group gathered around her and walked across the room, nodding to the people taking champagne glasses and oysters on the half shell from the silver trays the waiters passed. She moved to a quiet corner where Emma Laughten and Sophie stood alone.

"My dress is just as gorgeous as you described it to me. I can never thank you enough."

"Thank me by letting me make your wedding dress when you marry that Frenchman of yours. All the ladies in the room are swooning over him."

"Oh, dear, am I swooning, too?" Hannah laughed.

"Mother's right," Sophie chimed in. "You two make a handsome couple."

"Ah, we'll see. Perhaps I'm not right for him." Hannah turned to beckon a passing waiter. He stopped and refilled all their glasses.

"Surely all these men will become your customers," Sophie said. Excitement flushed her face after taking a sip of champagne. Look over at the door, Governor Bigler and his entourage have just come in."

Hannah beamed. "What do you think of *Maison de Paris*, Sophie? It isn't quite what we envisioned the first time we talked, is it? Not a humble cafe. Do you like the new name?"

"Better," Sophie said. "A romantic escape from the rush of the City. The orchestra on the balcony is such a fine touch. Gentlemen will bring their ladies here to impress them."

"You've thought of everything, Hannah," Emma said. "The frescos on the walls are beautiful. I could only wish Mister Laughten were alive to be here with me tonight."

Craning her neck to look around the room and primping at her hair, Sophie asked, "Do you think Pádraig will be here?"

"I'm sure he will. He promised to invite all the important men he knows."

Just at that moment Pádraig was coming through the doorway. Sophie's jaw dropped, and a dark scowl descended over her face, when she saw he had Nanette on his arm. She took another big sip from her glass, set it down and charged over to them.

"The likes of you don't belong in a respectable place like this. Look at you! Your breasts are climbing out of your dress. Why are you here?"

"The likes of me, is it? I've as much right to be here, escorted by Pádraig, as anybody." Nanette giggled. "We've already planned to dine in one of the private rooms when the restaurant is open. I hear there are couches up there. You and your mother can dine down on the main floor with all the other plain, lonely women of San Francisco."

Sophie didn't back off. She put her hands on her hips and stared at Nanette's bosom. "I'll bet every man here tonight recognizes that little freckle. They see it all the time at Pacific House."

"You little Irish bitch. You don't know anything. I'm not one of the girls at Pacific House. I'm better than that. Pádraig takes care of me now. He's an important man in the Democratic Party, and he's got no time for a plain Irish lass like you, or any other woman for that matter. Run along back to your mother. Let Pádraig and me enjoy this evening together."

While Sophie and Nanette were trading insults, Pádraig backed off a few steps and stood beside Miette, watching her greet others coming through the door. She fluttered her lashes and gave him a sweet smile.

"Monsieur, I have seen you before, but we have not been introduced. I am Miette. What is your name?"

"Pádraig Duggan."

"And will you dine here when we are open, Pádraig Duggan?"

"I plan to, Miette."

"Then it will be my special privilege to take care of you. I am an owner of *Maison de Paris*."

"I thought Hannah was the owner."

"Oh, well, Monsieur, she is a part owner, too. I see you have a lovely French girl accompanying you this evening..."

Nanette turned away from Sophie to confront Miette. "*S'éloigner de lui, petite chienne tu sale,*" she almost hissed.

Without missing a beat, Miette smiled back sweetly. "Little bitch, is it? Don't I know you from Les Halles, showing your titties to every man who passed?"

"Just stay away." Nanette took Pádraig's arm and led him away from both Sophie and Miette.

Heads turned as Pádraig and Nanette made their way through the growing crowd. He spoke a few words to David Scannell, the new fire chief, then saw a man of medium height, with a high forehead and a shock of red hair, speaking to a woman Pádraig did not recognize. He went directly up to him.

"Good evening, Captain Sherman. I see you've come back to us."

"I'm a civilian now. Resigned my commission." He turned to the attractive woman beside him. "This is Missus Jessie Benton Frémont. She just came into town from Las Mariposas, her home in the foothills, so I've brought her along. Captain Frémont's back east."

Pádraig took Jessie Frémont's hand and bowed over it. "It is an honor to meet you, Ma'am. I do so admire your husband. I am a free-soiler like yourselves."

Jessie Frémont thanked Pádraig with a warm smile. He turned back to Sherman. "What brings you back to California, sir?"

Before Sherman could answer Pádraig felt a sharp jab in his ribs. "Oh, and let me introduce Nanette," he said to Sherman and Jessie.

Sherman gave Nanette an admiring head to toe look. Jessie Frémont's look was not as warm. "Excuse me," she said and walked off

"There's money to be made here, and plenty of it, but not on an army salary," Sherman said. The Frémonts have their own gold mine, but I have to earn my share. I'm in the banking business now."

Across the room, Luc saw Governor John Bigler, Sam Brannan, Ramon d'Bouviere, and some other men he didn't know by name talking together. He walked over to join them.

"Good evening, gentlemen. I am Luc Benard," he introduced himself, nodding to the men he already knew. "I am pleased to welcome you to our new restaurant."

"Frenchman, are you?" Governor Bigler asked. "You've created a wonderful and authentic replication of Paris in our fair city, I must say."

"By birth I am, but I've been in your fine state since 1850, Governor."

"In the diggings, I suppose."

"There, and in the valley of the Napa River where I've bought some land and built a modest cabin."

"Then you intend to settle permanently?" one of the other men asked.

"A fine decision," Sam Brannan said when Luc nodded. "And what do you think of our City?"

"Fine, indeed. Although truth to tell I haven't had time to see it all. Busy getting *Maison de Paris* up and running, you know."

Bigler gazed around the large dining room, crowded now with well-wishers gathered in small knots, chatting and sipping champagne with friends. He showed the other men a broad grin. "We're still a bit shy of lovely ladies in our fine city though, aren't we? I would wager most all of the attractive women in San Francisco are gathered in this room tonight, and pitiful few they are."

"All but the better girls at Pacific House, where many of the men of the City take their pleasures," d'Bouviere said, smiling at the others.

"Well, I believe we're all gentlemen here," Bigler hurried to say, "so I can tell you I enjoy stopping in Pacific House when I'm in town. I've traveled a bit in my day and I can say quite fairly that Ipo has some of the best whores I've ever had the pleasure of knowing."

The others chuckled at the governor's word play. They exchanged comradely smiles with each other.

"Certainly not like the sing-song girls in Chinatown, are they?" Sam Brannan took over the conversation. "It's almost as if those sorrowful Chinese girls are not of the same sex as the lovely young women at Pacific House."

A couple of the men nodded at Brannan's words, but all stayed quiet and a few faded away from the group.

"Terrible! Terrible!" Bigler said. "The way those young girls are treated like prisoners—slaves you might even say—is abhorrent. I wish we could clean up Chinatown. It's a stain on the state's good reputation."

"Always a boomer, ay, Governor?"

"For our fine state? Absolutely."

"You'll never do anything about those poor girls, Governor," one of the other men said. "The Chinese live like animals. No different here than in Canton, as far as I can see. Best thing we can do is look the other way and let the Chinese treat their own however they choose."

Luc motioned to Hannah to join him and turned to Sam Brannan. At Pádraig's urging Brannan had become an investor in *Maison de Paris*. His wealth had come from selling picks, pans and shovels to the miners flooding into the foothills in '49 and '50, but now he was a big owner of San Francisco real estate.

"Thank you for your investment in our restaurant," Hannah told him coming into the group, as Governor Bigler and a couple of the other men walked off.

"It was my pleasure and a sound investment," Brannan said. "Do I remember you as the frightened young woman on the steamer to Stockton back in 1850? Look at you now."

Hannah blushed. "You have a good memory, sir. I was a frightened girl, indeed, trying to find my way to Angels Camp."

She turned to Ramon d'Bouviere. "*Bonsoir* Monsieur d'Bouviere. I am glad you could join us."

"Hannah and I are so appreciative of the confidence you've expressed in our new venture," Luc added.

"I came by with Emma and Sophie several times for your wonderful berry pies," he reminded her. "I hope you will continue to serve them."

"Indeed we will," Hannah said grinning. "Our specialty. In fact, the waiters will start passing trays of fruit pies in a few minutes."

"Your cherry pies are my favorite." D'Bouviere instinctively put his finger to his lip.

"Berry pies will always be our trademark."

As Hannah was talking she saw Senator William Gwin being greeted by Miette at the door. Four or five of his hangers-on followed him. She darted a glance at Jessie Frémont across the room and saw her hide a scowl.

D'Bouviere turned to a woman standing at his side. "This is another good friend," he introduced her. "She came to California long before the war from the island of Oahu. Her name is Ipo. She has a gambling establishment here in the City where I have my faro table."

Ipo was dressed in a tight-fitting gown of silver silk. She smiled warmly at Hannah and took Luc's hand when he extended it. Hannah's expression froze for an instant, her eyes narrowed and her jaw clenched, but she quickly regained her happier countenance. "It is a pleasure, Ipo," she said.

Ipo turned to Luc. "Might I have a short, private conversation with you, sir?"

Hannah raised her eyebrows.

"Not to worry, Hannah," d'Bouviere tried to reassure her.

"I will only keep you away from this lovely woman you so obviously admire for a moment, Mister Benard. It is only a little thing I need your opinion about."

"How can I be of service," Luc asked as they moved off a few feet.

"I am told you are responsible for the champagne tonight. It is the best in the City by far. Soon all of the men in San Francisco will be demanding it so I would like to buy several hundred bottles from you. Do not worry. Cost will be no problem. I will pay in gold on delivery."

Luc looked admiringly at the smooth coconut brown complexion of her face and neck. "So you are the mistress of Pacific House—is that the right word? Brut champagne is new, and you are correct, soon no one will drink sweet champagne any longer. My supplies will be limited for a while, but I will see what I can do. I'll bring some bottles to your place of business for you to sample the next time I am in San Francisco."

"We would be pleased to have you as our guest," Ipo said, giving him a kind of wink.

Luc laughed. "Thank you, but no need, it will be strictly business." He led her back to Hannah and d'Bouviere and another woman who had joined them. D'Bouviere introduced her as Lola Montez, an actress recently come to the City.

Nanette slipped away from Pádraig as he continued talking with Billy Sherman. She waited until there was a lull in the flow of guests coming in from the street and then went to Miette's side.

"It is silly for us to fight, you and me. We are the same really."

Miette stared into Nanette's face with a blank expression. She waited.

"We are both beautiful French women who know our way in the world. Beautiful French women are much sought after in San Francisco now and we are the prettiest ones here. Perhaps there is much gold in that for us."

"What are you suggesting?"

"Look around, *Chèrie*. See how popular this French restaurant is going to be. Where will men go after a fine meal here?"

"So?"

"So doesn't that give you any ideas? Think of an establishment with only French girls, along the lines of Pacific House. One could do well, I think. If you understand my words."

"I understand well enough. And how would the Madam at Pacific House like that?"

"Not too much. But what could she do? Her time has come and gone. The girls at Pacific House are old and worn out. None are as beautiful as I am, not even as pretty as you. I was Ipo's number one girl until I moved in with Pádraig"

"You would employ only French whores then?"

"*Oui*. We could bring them over from Paris."

"And where would you house them?"

Nanette slowly glanced around the room. "I don't know, but I am sure we could find a place like this one. You have upstairs rooms, no?"

"We live on the top floor and use the second floor rooms for private dining. But why go to all this trouble? Aren't you content with Pádraig?"

"He's good enough, but I want more. And I can have both. With Pádraig I always have to nag him to give me money to buy the things I want. He's difficult, but I manage. Are you sleeping with the Frenchman?"

By now the waiters were circulating the room with trays of fruit pie slices on plates. The crowd gathered for the grand opening clapped and raved as they took their first bites of the cherry, apple, blueberry, strawberry and boysenberry pies baked in a light, flaky crust.

Senator William Gwin, surrounded by his followers, was speaking to Governor John Bigler in hushed tones. His wife stood off to the side asking Hannah who her dressmaker was and if she could borrow her. The glow of the gaslights on the wall cast the two women in soft shadows, and the lights on the chandelier put sparkling highlights in their well coiffed hair and reflected

Their Golden Dreams

on the jewelry they wore. Senator Gwin kept looking about, trying to spot Pádraig. When he did—talking with young friends of his who had just arrived—Gwin broke off the conversation with Bigler, saying, "I need to speak with Duggan," and walked across the room to confront him, followed by Charles Grenough, his right hand man.

"Duggan. I saw you talking with Missus Frémont earlier," he started without waiting for Pádraig to end his conversation with one of the other men. "Now you're with this cadre of your firehouse buddies. If you think for one minute you can take over the Party by currying favor with Frémont or these people forget it. I am in control, not you."

"I am not interested in taking over the Party, Senator, only in making sure no slaves are brought into California."

"Soon you will bow to the inevitable. The Democratic Party controls San Francisco and San Francisco controls the state. Ay, Grenough?" He turned to the man at his side for acknowledgement "We bide our time for now, don't we? When the time is right you can be assured Negros will be brought here, Duggan. Look how the court ruled that the darky working in the diggings was still a slave, not a freeman, even though his master had brought him to a free state. Others will follow and soon it will be a flood that no laws can stop."

"Don't be so sure. Indeed, you've stacked the courts with your Chiv buddies. And yes, your pawn judge denied the black man his freedom, but each week more Northerners get off the Pacific Mail ships. When put to a vote slavery will lose."

Grenough and several other of Gwin's men took steps toward Pádraig. Gwin waved them off. "Watch your tongue with me, Duggan. I run the Party, not you or your free soil buddies. Certainly not Frémont. You could bring serious harm to yourself and these misguided men who look up to you if you are not careful. We might have our men in the southern part of the state petition Congress to become a separate territory. If we asked them to, a new state would welcome slaves. One way or the other California will join the South."

"A sad day that would be, Senator. Our strength is here in the north. If the southern part of the state voted for slavery war would surely follow. And the South would still not have access to our gold. Working men will never see slaves in the mines, I promise you that."

On his way to join Hannah and Jessie Frémont, Luc stopped by the front door to talk with Miette. "I think we're off to a good start," he said. "These people will surely come to dine and then tell others. But I think we are just about finished for the night, don't you? No need for you to stay by the door any longer, Miette."

She gave him her warmest smile. "It's all because of you, Luc. Hannah was floundering before you came back. Losing money. Without your plan I don't think she would have been able to rescue this business. Your contacts in France have helped create an authentic French-style restaurant. And the champagne is the best I've ever tasted."

Luc entertained a quick grin at her compliments. "You are too kind, mademoiselle. But I think you underestimate Hannah. Don't be too harsh on her. She was the one who raised all the money that made what I did possible. She believes in what we are doing and she manages the business well."

Miette kept her smile, showing her dimpled cheek and sparkling dark eyes. She turned her head up to him in a coquettish fashion, tossing about the black curls framing her face. "Don't misunderstand. I would never hurt Hannah. Perhaps we should celebrate our success. I have put away a chilled bottle of your champagne."

Later that evening, when the string quartet had stopped playing and the gas lamps and chandelier had been turned down, and the guests had departed raving about the new restaurant, Luc sat with Hannah sipping a final glass of champagne and recounting the successes of the evening.

"Everyone complimented the champagne," Hannah said, setting her glass down and reaching out to take Luc's hand. "How did you ever find it?"

He paused only a moment. "I was lucky. I know someone in Épernay who put me on to the new style." He rested his hand on top of hers. "Some day I want to take you to France with me to meet people there and see how beautiful our countryside is—all rolling hills and open valleys covered in lush vineyards, and the Marne River flowing gently through it."

"Wouldn't that be wonderful? I'd like that. But now I have a restaurant to run and a staff to manage."

"I think some problems with the staff may lie ahead for you."

"Miette?"

"Yes."

"Don't worry about her. Miette is more than staff to me, you know. She came to me as Parker was dying and she's stayed with me ever since. She has her ways, but she is very loyal to me."

Luc stayed quiet a moment, looking around the semi-dark room and watching the play of light from the street lamps outside on the walls, casting a glow on Hannah's pale skin. He squeezed her hand. "We are a wonderful pair, you and I. We fit together in so many ways. I always want to be by your side. I love you, Hannah."

"And I love you, too."

"Before too long I will have to go to France. I want you to come with me."

"If only I could. But it will take time for things to settle down enough for me to be away that long. A year at least. You should go by yourself when you need to."

"I don't think you understand what I am saying. I want you to come with me as my wife. I want to marry you, Hannah."

Hannah hesitated. "That would be wonderful, Luc, wouldn't it."

"Then you are saying yes?"

"No, Luc. The time isn't right, but I do love you so much. If you go to France without me I will be afraid you might never come back, and I don't know what I would do, but marriage scares me. I've always lost the people I love. I'm afraid to lose you."

CHAPTER 14

1855

PÁDRAIG WAS UNCOMFORTABLE riding in the carriage. He would have preferred to walk about the city conducting his business because he felt closer to the workingmen when he did, but Nanette insisted they go by carriage, even short distances, whenever she accompanied him. To do less, she said, was a sign of disrespect to her, and lowered their standings in the eyes of San Franciscans.

"Look at me," she said as they rode toward Fire Station Six's engine house, "I am a sorry sight to be seen by those men."

"Sorry sight? You are one of the most beautiful women in the City. Look how that dress shows off your figure that I love so much to hold. You are perfect."

"Far from it! I could be prettier if I were better dressed. You keep me in rags, Pádraig."

"Are we talking about this again?"

"It's important for me to look my best when I accompany you to these meetings."

"What's important, Nanette, is that I keep the men's support. Most of them at Fire Six came from Baltimore and farther south. We need them on our side."

"Exactly. If you dressed me better it would make a stronger impression on them. I need a new frock. Two would be better still. You haven't bought me anything new in weeks."

"I'm doing the best I can. I'll buy you a new dress soon."

"And when will that be, pray tell?" She sat forward on the carriage seat, probing him with narrowed eyes and a straightened brow. The auburn ringlets of her hair were bouncing up and down on the sides of her face as she grew more agitated.

"Soon, I promise."

"You always promise. I am devoting all my time to you. You are the only man allowed in my bed, and yet you treat me as if I am nothing. I'm not nothing, Pádraig! Think how lucky you are to have me. You just said I'm one of the most beautiful women in San Francisco, but do you treat me that way? No, you don't! Maybe I made a mistake with you."

Pádraig stayed quiet.

"Well?" she demanded.

"Well what? I said I would buy you a new dress as soon as I can."

"I need more jewelry, too."

When the carriage stopped in front of the fire station, he was glad to be out of it. Nanette straightened her ruffled dress and quickly pinched her cheeks to add some color. She offered the entire group of assembled men a seductive smile as she entered.

But Pádraig stopped short in the doorway when he saw Senator William Gwin and a group of his followers already inside, standing by the hose wagon surrounded by firemen.

Gwin spotted him and shouted across the big room. "What are you doing here, Duggan?"

"Same as you, Senator, wanting to speak to the men on behalf of the Party."

"Not the same certainly. These are men from the South. They share my views, not yours."

"San Francisco's workingmen don't support slavery, Senator. Not if it costs them their jobs."

Their Golden Dreams

"You've a strong following among them, Duggan, and we need their support, but you are misled because you have no vision for the future of California."

"With all respect, Senator, the California constitution outlawed slavery."

"That was only to get us into the Union. We can change the constitution with enough votes. Or we could divide California in two, with slavery allowed in the south, as I've told you before. All that is possible, and these men of the Chivalry standing beside me will work to make it happen."

There was a rumble of dissent from the firemen gathered around the hose wagon that faded away just as quickly as it had started.

"Why would any miners working the diggings in the foothills allow themselves to be displaced by your rich southern friends' slaves? Or work alongside them for that matter. Think about it, Senator, that's no different than these firemen losing their jobs if slave owners brought darkies into the City. They'd fight it. Just ask these men."

There was a stirring among the firemen. Pádraig knew most of them. They were his friends, good workers. He didn't think they supported Gwin, but they were too respectful to question him.

"Watch out you're not on the losing side of this, Duggan," Gwin called out, his voice rising. Some of his cronies began moving toward Pádraig. Nanette retreated to the doorway. "The Party can't go much longer divided like this. Look at the men I brought with me today. They control city jobs. We are strong. It is inevitable our policies will win out."

"For you it's power and politics, Senator, for me it's these men. I came from New York's Lower East Side—the Bowery—I saw how corrupt politicians could be. I'll stand up for the rights of our workers and... "

"Watch your tongue! Things could go badly for you."

With that, the Senator nodded to Charles Grenough, then turned on his heels and left the fire station. Grenough and a half dozen of the men with him immediately surrounded Pádraig and hustled him out the rear door to the back of the station, before any of the Station Six men could come to his aid. Nanette followed them out, an expression of disgust on her face. She stood far off to the side. Several of Grenough's men peeled off from the others and shut the door keeping the firemen inside. Pádraig could hear his friends pounding and shouting as they tried to come to his rescue, but they couldn't get to him because Grenough's bullies were holding the door shut.

A barrel-shaped man with piercing, bulging eyes, Grenough grabbed Pádraig's arm. "It's a big mistake to talk that way to the Senator, Duggan. A big mistake. We need to educate you."

Pádraig never saw Grenough's blow coming. It hit him in the side of the head and sent him reeling into the arms of the other men. Nanette watched wide-eyed as they began pummeling him. Throwing him back and forth from one side of the circle to the other, they shouted and swore at him, calling him nigger-lover, traitor and stinkin' abolitionist among other things. He had no defense from the fists and knees and boots assaulting him. They threw him on the ground and continued hitting and kicking him, shouting and cursing for several more minutes.

"That's enough," Grenough shouted. "Lets get out of here." Abruptly, the ruffians were gone, vanishing at a run out of the alley, on to the street and around a corner, leaving Pádraig lying on the ground. Little trickles of blood ran from the corner of his mouth and cuts on his face and arms. His ribs ached. He stayed on the ground, unable to get up, hardly able to move. He lay there only a few moments before the firemen of Station Six bolted through the door and were at his side, shocked at the sight of the brutality of the attack. They carefully helped him to an old bench by the rear door. One of the men ran back inside the station and returned with a bowl of water and towels. They tended to his wounds as best they could.

Nanette came to stand in front of him, looking down at his battered face. She let out a low moan, not a scream, more of an animal sound deep in her throat.

He looked at her with an expression of helplessness, in too much pain to talk.

She kept staring at him for several moments before speaking. "I won't stay with you, Pádraig," she said with a scornful voice. "You are a fool and a loser. I see I have made a bad choice. I need a man who will protect me and give me the things I want, not lie on the ground beaten within an inch of his life. I'm leaving you. I'm going to find Charles Grenough. He looks like a man who knows how to treat a beautiful woman. These men can take care of you, I am leaving." Then she turned her back and walked off.

After a while, when he had recovered his strength sufficiently, two of the firemen each took one of his arms around their shoulder and slowly escorted him to his lodgings.

CHAPTER 15

1856

"THE PRIVATE ROOMS are all reserved for tonight," Miette told Hannah. They were seated in the empty dining room, going over the coming evening's reservations while staff moved around setting tables and talking with each other in lowered voices. "Sam Brannan has one room and Charles Grenough another. Most of the main floor tables are reserved too. I told the chef to order in more food. We should have a full restaurant."

"Wonderful. You're doing a fine job, Miette. I think it's the warm, personal way you treat our customers that keeps them coming back."

Miette blushed. "In Paris I learned my life could be easier if I smiled. It didn't matter how I felt inside as long as people saw me smile. Now it is a habit."

"How do you really feel then? Are you just putting on a pretty face to please our dinner guests?" Hannah asked.

"Certainly not, Madame." Miette's voice was tinged with pique. She stopped writing in the reservation book, put her pencil down, and looked directly at Hannah. "I am about as happy as I ever dreamed of being. Our restaurant is a success beyond my wildest imaginings. My share of the profits grows each night. I sleep soundly—not like I did in Paris."

"About as happy?" Hannah gave her a probing look.

"Of course there are still things I hope for. But I am content enough without them."

"Like a family?"

"*Oui*. But a woman with a past life like mine can hardly expect to find a man who would accept her for a wife."

"Is that the way it is with the young man who's been coming around to see you lately?"

"Seth? I don't know. Seth is very nice, but I don't expect too much from him. That way I will not be disappointed if he stops calling on me. He's a farmer from Iowa, did I tell you that? I don't even know where Iowa is. Do you?"

Hannah laughed. "Not really. On the other side of the mountains somewhere, in the middle of the country maybe, I'm not sure either. There's a lot of empty space between Boston and California."

"He's nice enough for now, but not like Luc Benard. Monsieur Benard is a fine, handsome gentleman. Look at all he has done for us."

"We owe our good fortune to him. Without his help *Maison de Paris* would never have become a success."

"Do you ever think about marrying him, Madame? Starting a family together?"

"I do. Sometimes. But I am happy with the way things are. Like you, I guess. I am here in the City and Luc has his vineyard in Napa. We're together when he comes to town, which is more often these days."

"Lovers?"

"Yes, lovers."

"You don't want more?"

"Like you, I try to live one day at a time. He might decide to leave me and I couldn't do anything to keep him. Most of the people in my life have left me. I've learned not to expect anything different, that way I am not disappointed."

Miette nodded understanding. They sat together in the empty restaurant hardly aware of the pleasant aromas coming from the kitchen, each absorbed in her own thoughts.

When Luc Benard hurried through the door a few minutes later, briefly blocking the light coming in, their reveries ended. He was dressed in a dark frockcoat and top hat, with a brightly colored cravat at his neck and a light tan-colored waistcoat. His dark face held a smile and his eyes twinkled.

"*Bonjour, mademoiselles.*"

"*Bonjour, Monsieur.* We were only now talking about you."

"Probably wondering when your next bottles of champagne would arrive, like all my other customers."

"If they don't arrive soon we'll be out."

"Soon, I hope, but that is why I have come to speak with you, Hannah."

"Only that?" Miette teased.

Luc grinned. "Well no, Miette," He approached the table. "If you don't mind I would like to speak privately with Hannah."

She gave him a questioning glance then nodded to Miette, who laughed softly. Gathering up her book and seating chart she rose from the table. She gave Luc a parting look that came close to a wink. When she had gone back to the kitchen, his face saddened. Hannah waited for him to start.

"I received a letter from France. It came on the morning ship. My mother writes me that my father has died."

"Oh, my dear. I am so sorry for you."

"Naturally, I will have to go back to Épernay for awhile."

"Of course you must. To be with her."

"I would like you to come with me."

"That wouldn't be right. You should devote yourself to your mother in her time of mourning."

"It is a little more complicated than that. I don't know how long I will have to stay."

"I understand, Luc. I will miss you." The familiar emptiness started in her stomach again.

"Please come with me."

She trembled just slightly. "No, I think it's best that I stay here."

"Hannah, I am pleading with you to come with me. The fact is I might never be able to return to California. I can't bear the thought of losing you again. When you left Angels Camp I was beside myself missing you. Now that I've found you again... what I am saying is that I love you and want to take you to France as my wife."

His words stunned her. She felt tightness in her chest, difficulty taking a breath. Rising from the table too stunned to speak, she stood in back of her chair as if it were a barricade. He waited and watched her. She walked away from him, going to the doorway and looking out at the people passing by on the sidewalk. For a long time she just stood there, her back to him.

"How could I possibly leave?" she said at last over her shoulder. "Miette couldn't manage without me."

"Miette would do just fine. But that's not important. That's only your way of avoiding my proposal. You and I are what's important, not the restaurant. I am capable of caring for you the rest of our lives and you already have a fortune from *Maison de Paris*. And we've both already lost someone we loved. If you refuse me now, you may never have another chance at happiness. Nor I. Please, Hannah, I'm begging you. I love you."

All the memories of all the pain of all the people who had left her over all the years flooded though her mind. Tears ran down her cheeks. This time is different, she told herself. This time I am abandoning him. I can't. Turning, she took a small, hesitant step toward him. Then another. Then she ran into his arms, burying her head in his chest.

"I don't want to be alone anymore. I do love you, Luc. Take me with you wherever you go. I won't lose you again."

⸺

The next two months were a blur of joyous activity, starting with their wedding at Old Saint Mary's Cathedral on Dupont and California Streets, where Bishop Joseph Alemany conducted the nuptial service.

"How did you get the bishop to marry us on such short notice?" she asked her new husband when they were alone that night.

He gave her a contented smile and reached out to touch the soft skin of her bare shoulder. "It was nothing, *Chèrie*. The bishop is a Frenchman. We Frenchmen understand love, so we understood each other."

"Will you always take such good care of me?" She inched her body closer to him.

"I plan to. You deserve nothing but the best."

"I love you so much, Luc..."

The rest of her words were lost as he took her in his arms and covered her with kisses.

At first reluctant, Miette soon warmed to the idea of taking over the restaurant. It was Hannah who had trouble letting go.

"Look, Hannah," Luc told her, "San Francisco is no longer growing by leaps and bounds as it was a couple of years ago. Miette should have no trouble as long as she keeps a good chef in the kitchen."

"I do worry about her, even though I know how capable she is."

"*Maison de Paris* has been good to both of us. But it's only a restaurant—they come and go. No need for you to concern yourself about it. I've never met a woman more motivated by

Their Golden Dreams

money than Miette so let her have your share. Look how she greets the customers? They feel as if this beautiful young French woman is seducing them. I have no doubt she'll succeed."

"You've earned enough from the champagne business to provide for us?"

"In a manner of speaking I have. George Yount will take care of the Napa vineyard—he's a good farmer. In time I might sell it to him."

"The way you're talking it sounds like we might never return."

He shrugged. "Time will tell."

With Miette settled in her new role, Luc booked passage on the steamship *Golden Gate* for Panama, the first leg of their long journey to France. When they reached New York they boarded the American Collins Line steamer *Baltic*.

"I've reserved one of their honeymoon cabins for us," he told Hannah.

She blushed.

They crossed the Atlantic in style. Their cabin was lavishly furnished in satinwood and draped with damask curtains. It had a sofa and two washbasins and smelled of lemon oil. Just outside was the grand salon, with floor to ceiling stained glass windows and a skylight. Richly carpeted, it was filled with rose, satin and olive wood furniture, with Italian marble tables. Each evening they dressed formally for dinner and dined surrounded by a hundred other beautifully attired travelers.

"Last year the *Baltic* made the fastest Atlantic crossing, beating all the Cunard Line steamers," he told her with a burst of pride one evening.

"The way you go on you'd think you were the captain." Then, smiling warmly across the table at him, she said, "I don't want this wonderful honeymoon to ever end."

He gave her a playful grin. "It will take awhile. We have plenty of time to be together. Another four days to Liverpool, then a train to Folkstone and a steamer across the English Channel. Another train to Paris, where we will spend a night before going on to Épernay." He paused and looked thoughtfully at her for several moments. "I am sad my father won't be there to meet the beautiful young woman I've married. I'm so happy to have you with me I forget it will be a sad occasion when we arrive. But I know my mother will like you."

"I hope I can live up to her expectations. Yours, too."

In France, they rode the train from Boulogne through the town of Amiens to Paris. It rained much of the way with heavy clouds submerging the landscape in a smoky gray mist. Exhausted as she was from over a month of travel, the mood outside the train did nothing to improve her spirits. She looked at the sights of Paris they were passing as the horse-drawn carriage took them from the station to the hotel, and found nothing charming. She tried to hide her disappointment, but Luc noticed.

He took her hand in an effort to reassure her. "Paris is being rebuilt. The Emperor has ordered it. He promises a beautiful modern city when the work is completed in another few years."

"And in the meantime?"

He shrugged. "Many of the lower working class are being displaced by the construction. Their lodgings are being torn down."

"Where do they go?"

"I don't know. I guess they find new places or move away."

After a night in a bed that didn't rock or sway, Hannah was in a better mood the next morning as they boarded the train. As the steam locomotive left the station there were clouds racing across the sky, leaving it dark and threatening one minute and bathed in bright sunlight that made the city sparkle the next.

Their Golden Dreams

She stared out the window as the train lurched along, belching black smoke, with an acrid odor that occasionally found its way into their compartment. Luc sat beside her, holding her hand and pointing out everything they passed. Brick red and pale yellow foliage growing along the tracks seemed to dance in the whirlwind of the passing.

Traveling north and east, the land became a series of rural valleys embraced by wooded hills. Fields had already given up their yearly bounty and now, in shades of brown and gold, they were resting, awaiting a warming blanket of snow before the next spring. Small homes, some whitewashed stucco and some stone, capped by red roofs, nested against the base of the hills. She studied them as they sped past.

As they progressed, the forests retreated higher up the slopes and the lower elevations were cloaked in vineyards. Mostly unseen in the distance, only peeking out from behind the trees at infrequent intervals, a gentle river flowed westward.

"The Marne," he told her. "It flows through the heart of Épernay. We'll soon be home."

Home. Hannah played with the word in her head. It wouldn't matter how small it was or how modest, she told herself, as long as they were together. She would never let go of him.

Épernay perched on a hilltop overlooking the river. A lone carriage waited outside the almost deserted station as they disembarked. Luc was surprised to see a man waving to him from the driver's bench. Laughing, he grabbed Hannah's arm and pointed. "That old gentleman works for our family. He's come to greet us. *Bonjour*, Emile," he shouted.

"*Bonjour. Je suis venu à la station chaque jour d'attente pour vous.*"

Hannah looked at Luc.

"He says he has come to the station every day to await us since mother received my letter."

"Your mother must be anxious to have you home." Hannah smiled a greeting to Emile and took Luc's arm as they walked to the carriage.

Showing her a welcoming grin that revealed several missing teeth and a slight whiff of garlic, Emile extended his hand to assist her up the step onto the rear seat. Then he collected the trunks and traveling satchels from the station platform and loaded them in back of the carriage. He climbed on the driver's bench, clucking to the horse. "*Fouler*," he commanded and they began to climb the hill into the town. They circled a tall column topped by a statue of Napoleon, with the town's imposing stone church just off to the right, before continuing up the hill. Near the top the carriage stopped.

"We are here," Luc told her.

"Here?"

"My father's house. Where we will live."

She thought the three-story mansion brooding behind an ornate iron fence and gate was more like a fairy book castle than a home. Built of brick, with stone trim, the massive building was anchored by a central tower and flanked by other towers at each end. The lower levels had arched floor-to-ceiling windows with decorative stonework surrounds. A slate mansard roof capped the structure, with chimneys rising above it. On each side of the main house, and reaching to the street, were twin brick buildings. The whole façade presented a U-shaped fortress that dominated the street from behind the protective iron fence.

Her heart raced.

Looking just a bit smug, Luc took her gloved hand and sat silently beside her while she tried to digest the grandeur and monumental style of the building.

She felt the strength of his hand, but hers went limp. She had trouble taking a breath. "Your father's house?"

"Our home now." He climbed down from the carriage and helped to steady her descent to the cobblestoned street. "Shall we go inside to meet my mother?"

"No." She shook off his hand in a sudden, violent gesture. Taking a firm grip on the side of the carriage, she glared at him. "I'm not moving until you explain to me what this is all about."

Startled, he motioned to Emile, who had started unloading the baggage, to step away. The old gentleman joined a small knot of men who had emerged from one of the buildings along the street, and stood off to the side of the courtyard. Hannah climbed back into the carriage and sat staring straight ahead, gripping the side rail in her left hand. Luc got back in beside her, confusion etched on his face. "I see now that this has come as a shock to you. Let's go inside so I can introduce you to Mother. Then I'll explain it all."

"No. I won't go anywhere until you do explain. Obviously you are not what you seemed to be in California. You have misled me."

"What I am was not important in California. Everyone there was an adventurer. We were all equal."

"It looks as if you are more equal than the rest of us. I've never lived in fairytale castles like this. I am not a princess."

"I didn't want anyone at the diggings to know my background. I wanted to be accepted on my own, not because of my family."

"Your family appears to be very rich. Are you nobility? Some kind of French prince or count? Have I accidentally married a prince then? Tell the truth, Luc."

He squeezed her hand. She pulled it away.

"I am sorry. I never meant to mislead you. I love you and I wanted you to love me for me, not for money, not for my family. We are certainly not aristocrats. My father and his father have been successful merchants. We are *bourgeois*, but you will always be my princess."

She gave him a frosted look. "I loved you in Angels Camp when you were a scruffy, smelly, dirty miner like all the other men. Why didn't you trust me with the truth?"

"I never lied. I said I was working for a champagne merchant when the revolution broke out and wanted to come to California for an adventure. I told you that again the night at dinner when we talked about opening the restaurant. The merchant was my father. Would you have believed me then if I had described this house to you? It is a bit hard to believe, isn't it?"

Her face softened. As she let out a deep breath she felt her anxiety fade. She let go the carriage rail she had been gripping so tightly her hand ached. She turned to look at him with the hint of a smile starting. "When you had the carriage stop here I thought it was a trick—or a dream. Then for a moment I thought we weren't really married. I had a feeling you were going to get out, go inside and leave me sitting here. That doesn't make sense, I know, but I couldn't stand the thought of you leaving me. I thought I wasn't good enough for you when I saw this castle."

"Please don't call it a castle."

"Perhaps it is a castle and you are my prince. I'm sorry I doubted you. I'm ready to meet your mother."

"Not yet! I must tell you more so you won't think I'm holding back. First, I want to tell you about my family." He drew a breath and settled himself. Turning away from her for a moment, as if to gather his thoughts, he looked beyond the mansion where small slivers of the Marne gleamed silver between stands of alder and ash in the valley. On the far hillsides grape vines were beginning to die back, showing flashes of red and golden leaves.

Turning to her he spoke in a subdued voice. "My family

Their Golden Dreams

has lived here in the Champagne region as long as anyone can remember. They were peasant farmers and raised sheep, like the other families along the river. But my grandfather was a restless man. He left his wife with a young daughter and went to the Caribbean in the last century. With almost no money he used slave labor to start a sugar plantation on the island of Saint Dominque. One of the slave women became his mistress. She was my grandmother."

"Are you saying your grandmother was a black slave woman?"

"Does that shock you? A lot of French colonists in the Caribbean had black mistresses."

"You inherited some of her features."

"Perhaps, yes. My father was also dark." He stopped talking and studied her face, as if he were trying to read her thoughts. He waited to see if she would make further comment, but she stayed quiet, looking directly at him a long time before speaking.

"I'm glad you have told me. If you expected me to be put off by your Negro blood I am not. No more than you might be to learn I come from Irish peasant stock."

"My grandfather's mistress was pregnant with Achille, my father, when the slaves revolted on Saint Dominque. He brought her here and included her in his family. Strange as that might sound to you it wasn't that unusual at the time. When his wife produced no male heirs, he had my father declared his legal son to inherit the family estate. Together father and son began buying grapes from many of the farmers who had sold off their sheep when growing grapes became more profitable. Now that Achille has died the Champagne House of *Benard et fils*, and all that goes with it, like this mansion, have passed on to me. It will pass on to our children one day, Hannah. That is French law. Let's go inside now."

Luc's mother greeted them in a vestibule just off the front door. It was a small room with a high ceiling, ornate moldings and window treatments, and an old smell. She stood before a floor-to-ceiling mirror wearing a long gray dress with rows of flounces over several petticoats. Hannah thought the dress out of date and that the ringlet curls on each side of her mother-in-law's aging face were the result of hair attachments.

"*Tu avez une belle mariée, Luc...*" the woman said, giving her a sharp appraisal while keeping a stern look on her Gallic face.

Hannah tugged at his arm. "What did she say?"

"She said you are a very pretty bride." He beamed his pleasure at his mother's acceptance.

"*...mais tu auriez pu trouver une belle jeune fille Française,*" the old woman continued.

Hannah saw Luc flinch. "And that?"

He spoke sharply to his mother then grinned at her. "Oh, nothing. Mothers are always protective of their sons."

"It will be so hard for me to learn your language. Tell her I will try to make you a good wife." As she said it, she gave the old woman an unsmiling direct look.

CHAPTER 16

1856

BUNDLED UP IN a woolen manton over her dress against a chilling breeze, Hannah followed Luc out of the mansion. He put his arm around her, pulling her close beside him, and walked a little way down the hill behind the large house toward the river in the valley below.

"I heard you and your mother talking in raised voices last night," she asked him. "Were you arguing about me?"

"It was nothing. Things have changed since Father died. She managed the business until I arrived. But now I am in charge."

In an open space about a hundred yards above a small, square-built stone and brick house, with a steeply pitched roof, he stopped walking and pointed.

"The house down there is where I grew up. I wanted you to see it so you would know I didn't always live in such a grand manner. My grandfather only built the mansion for his wife when his business grew—to keep her happy and house his mistress in a separate wing. My father inherited it when his father died."

"Will your mother live in it with us now?"

"She will. At least for a time."

"Yesterday I got the feeling she was not pleased with me."

"Mother has old fashioned ideas. She wanted a French bride for me. Don't worry, she will get used to you."

"Not a very positive way to put it."

"Give her some time. Mother has never been a happy person. She and Father argued frequently. Often as a boy I came here to sit and look out at the valley to get away from their quarreling. She was always hard on me." Staring across the open expanse at the far hillside across the river, he grabbed her arm and pointed. "There, can you see the wagon? They are hurrying to finish the harvest before the frost shuts the vines down for the winter. In Le Champagne it is always a struggle to get the grapes picked. It is not such a good climate for grape-growing here, the grapes never fully ripen in our cool, short summers. But then that is the secret of our champagne—that and the poor soil that forces the grapes to struggle."

Hannah pulled the manton tight to her neck and buried her chin against the shiver she felt. Clouds scudded from the east while she stood looking at the tiny figures of men loading baskets of grapes into a bin on the wagon. She gave Luc no hint of her discomfort except to take his hand and lean close to him. "Show me where your vineyards are. Can we see them from here?"

"Our vineyards? Oh, *mon cher*, we have no vineyards. We don't grow grapes, we buy then from growers all over the region. That wagon I pointed to—as soon as it is loaded it will start down the hill. It might come up here to the House of Benard et fils or one of the other champagne houses in Épernay or even go to Reims."

She was thoughtful a moment, still straining to see across the valley. "There is so much for me to learn."

He bent to kiss her cheek. As he did a slight queasy feeling in her stomach came and went.

"It is time for you to start. I must ride into Reims today to our *notaire*—you say attorney—about protecting my inheritance." He took a last look out over the valley at the distant vineyards and then at the little stone house. "Come with me. I will introduce you to our *Chef de Cave*."

"What about your inheritance?"

"Mother is questioning it. So I think we need to have an agreement in writing that clearly names you as my wife and heir."

She gave him an apprehensive look but decided to keep her thoughts private. Still huddled together, they walked back toward the mansion. But instead of going in, he led her to the large building flanking it on the left. On the street a horse-drawn wagon was unloading wooden bins of grapes. Inside, Emile and the other men she'd seen the day before were emptying them into a small crushing machine. The room was suffused with the smell of yeast and fermenting grapes that caught her by surprise and stayed a bit unpleasantly with her. Nearby, large wooden barrels with iron hoops were stacked almost to the ceiling.

A man came from a tiny office tucked at the back of the building where empty bins were stacked three high along the walls. He looked middle age, older than Luc, but not as old as Emile or the other workers feeding the gapes into the crusher. The worry lines around his eyes and mouth told of a life of responsibility, but a shock of unruly light brown hair and a broad grin softened his appearance.

"*Bonjour Monsieur Benard, Madame Benard.*" He bowed.

"*Bonjour* Camille." Luc spoke a few words in French, then changed to English, turning to her. "This is Camille André, our *Chef de Cave*. He has worked for my father since he was a young man, well before I was born. I will take on the responsibility for selling our champagne in Europe and America once we are settled, and he will oversee all aspects of our production."

She extended her hand to Monsieur André and then was embarrassed when he brushed it with his lips.

"I am pleased to meet you, Madame, and wish you and Monsieur Benard a long and happy married life."

She smiled at him, pleased he spoke English. "I hope we will get to know each other well, Mister André."

"I must ride into Reims now and won't return until late evening, so I have asked Camille to show you how we make our champagne. It's not like other wines, you know. It is very special. Camille knows how to coax the champagne out of the grapes. We count on him for our unique quality."

After Luc left Camille André turned to her with a look that told her he knew his skills well, but wasn't sure how to explain them to her in English.

"Monsieur Benard says I coax the champagne from the grapes. That is true, but as you can see it takes many men to assist me. It is a long process. Here you see just the start. Our grapes come from all over *Le Champagne*. After they are crushed I combine the juice from many vineyards and different vintages or harvests to create a cuvée—a blend you would say—that always has the special characteristic of the House of Benard. After the wine has fermented completely in the barrels you see stacked against the walls, we put it in bottles, but it is only still wine. If you come with me I'll show you how we put bubbles into it."

André led her away from the workers at the crusher to the back of the building where he stopped at the head of a descending stairway.

"I am very pleased that Luc has come back to us with such a pretty wife. We have missed him very much since his father died. I hear that you owned a successful restaurant in San Francisco that served our champagne."

"We owned it together."

Even away from the other workers André spoke in a quiet voice. "Things were not so good here before you arrived. Now they will be better."

"Why was that, Camille?"

"The widow Benard wanted to manage things." He stopped. "I should not speak of that, I apologize." He moved to the head of the stairs. "We will go down into the caves now."

As they started down, the rough-cut steps felt slippery. A little uncertain, she hesitated a moment then put her hand on André's arm to steady herself. At the bottom of the steps she saw they were at the head of a long, dim tunnel lit by oil lamps spaced along the walls. The feeble flames cast a dim orange light that kept the passageway from going completely dark. The smoke the lamps gave off created a haze. She was aware of an assortment of smells she couldn't identify that cloyed at her nose. Reaching out, she touched the wall and recoiled quickly, feeling its cold dampness that sent another shiver through her.

"The ground beneath most of the region is chalk," André told her. "The tunnels and caves are perfect for storing champagne as it ferments and ages. Many have been here for centuries—they were started by Roman slaves quarrying the chalk—but over the years more and more tunnels have been carved out."

The dimness gave Hannah a disquieting feeling that wouldn't leave her. "Can't you get lost in all these tunnels? It's very dark, isn't it?"

"I suppose you could. There are hundreds, maybe thousands of kilometers of tunnels around Épernay and Reims. Nobody knows how many. Our main tunnel has perhaps fifty or sixty branch tunnels. Some are dead ends, but our workers know their way around them."

He waited while their eyes adjusted to the light. She continued to feel unsettled. The low ceiling seemed to press down on her.

"I won't let you get lost, Madame, please do not concern yourself. Back when Achille was the head of the House of Benard he treated us like a family. I hope it can be that way with your husband. Please feel at ease to come to me whenever you have questions. Now I would like to show you what happens after the still wine has been put into the bottles with temporary caps and brought down here."

Starting slowly, he proceeded down the tunnel. The lamps on the walls gave off enough light for them to see fifteen or twenty feet ahead, but the smoke still irritated her eyes and throat. She followed him, staying close. Where the tunnel widened into a cavity in the chalk wall, he stopped and pointed to bottles stacked on their sides, head to foot between thin layers of wood. The stack filled the opening and rose toward the ceiling. She could see hundreds of bottles. There might have been even more, but the haze from the lamps kept her from seeing to the back of the cave, and the bottles seemed to shimmer in the faint light, not holding steady in her gaze.

"These bottles are going through their second fermentation. We have added a different yeast from the first fermentation and a bit of sugar to the wine and capped it. The bottles will rest here for several months or more, and the tiny bubbles are formed."

"Perhaps we should start back now, Camille. My stomach is not feeling right."

"One more thing to show you. Just around the corner up ahead. Then we will go back." André took a quick look at her face. "It's not unusual to feel unsettled the first time in the tunnels. We'll go back up as soon as I tell you about the riddling. It's very important."

He guided her along the tunnel. She went reluctantly, not wanting to offend him, but fighting a growing uneasy feeling in her stomach. They stopped at another cavity in the wall in front of a strange-looking device. Two racks made of wood set at angles to each other formed a kind of tent or pyramid with the floor. Each wooden side had rows of oblique holes cut into it. Bottles were inserted in each hole, neck first, its top angling down toward the floor.

"Here we are collecting the spent yeast and sugars in the neck of each bottle. We turn each one a little at a time and increase the angle so the bottles will wind up almost upside down over the next month or so. When all the wastes from the sugar and yeast are concentrated in the neck we submerge the bottle in ice water. Then we remove the cap. The residue is shot out of the bottle by the pressure inside. We add more wine and cork the bottle and put a wire cage on the cork for safety. So then it is ready to be sold and consumed."

The thought of ice water made her shiver again. She reached out a hand to steady herself on the tent-like structure that held the bottles, "I'm feeling a little dizzy."

"Oh, *s'il vous plait, Madame!*" André's hand quickly reached out to stabilize the wooden structure. "The bottles can explode if we are not careful, the glass of some is quite weak and there is much gas in every bottle." He looked at her face and his concern showed in his eyes. "I apologize, Madame. I have kept you too long. *Je suis désolé*, I am very sorry."

Hannah heard his words and tried to assure him with a smile, but it was a weak one and by now the tunnel was spinning around her. She looked for something to hold on to, but found only André's arm. She tipped forward, her head pressing against his chest. Then she fainted, crumpling into his arms.

CHAPTER 17

1856

MIETTE WAS MEETING with the chef about the *Maison de Paris* menu on a blustery December afternoon in San Francisco when Seth came through the door. Not to interrupt their conversation, he stood off to the side, pretending to study the frescos on the wall.

"We'll need to have a hearty dish on the menu as the nights get colder and rainier," she told the chef. "What did you prepare in Reims that we could serve here?"

"*Oui*, mademoiselle, a cassoulet of ham and chicken with small potatoes, vegetables and white beans in a red wine sauce, with a sausage tossed in to add a spicy flavor."

Miette agreed. They continued to talk several more minutes before the chef returned to the kitchen. Miette gave Seth a warm *bonjour* and beckoned him to join her at the table. "What is it that brings you here today?"

"To see you and invite you to go to a performance at the opera house with me on Sunday afternoon. Since the restaurant is closed I thought we could spend some time together."

Miette thought Seth a nondescript young man, perhaps a year or two her junior. He had the kind of long, lean, farm boy body that made his arms and legs seem out of proportion. A shock of white-blond hair escaped from his workingman's cap onto his forehead. He removed it and tried to brush his hair with the back of his hand.

"And what show will we see?"

"Oh, I forgot to say. Lotta Crabtree will sing and dance and play the banjo. It sounds like fun."

"And you'd like me to accompany you to the opera house? There will be a lot of people there who will see us."

"I'd be proud to have them see you with me. You're one of the handsomest gals in San Francisco. You're the prettiest I've ever seen, much prettier than any of the girls in Keokuk."

"Well, if you're sure then I'd be pleased to go with you, Seth."

"And after we could have a meal together. I've been saving my wages to take you out."

"Do you have a best girl back home?"

"I don't think I'll ever make it back to Iowa. This is my home now. More opportunity here if you're willing to work hard. Pádraig got me started and showed me the ropes."

As they were talking, a figure appeared in the doorway, filling it completely, blocking some of the afternoon sunlight and casting a shadow across the room. Miette glanced up. She stared hard to make out the silhouetted figure. It was Nanette she saw standing there, as if she were posing for a picture or waiting to be announced. The skirt of the gown she was wearing filled the doorway beyond its capacity to accommodate it, so Nanette was having some difficulty getting through. She tried to flatten it against her thighs with her hands, but each time she did the voluminous material billowed out in a different direction. For a moment it seemed she might be stuck.

Miette rose from the table, watching speechlessly with Seth, as Nanette finally got control of her skirt and made it into the room. She was tempted to make a comment, but held back.

"Isn't it magnificent?" Nanette asked, looking to her audience for approval. "It has a hoop." She rearranged the skirt so it formed a perfect bell shape, enclosing her from the waist down. The bodice was sparse by comparison. Not enough material had been used to cover the rise of her breasts, and the waist was pinched tight. "Well, aren't you going to say anything?"

Seth continued to stare. He could only nod his head.

"It's a beautiful dress." Miette finally got the words out. "But isn't it a bit early in the day for a ball gown?"

"I just had to put it on. It arrived from New Orleans this morning. Charles Grenough bought it as a token of the high esteem he holds me in. It must have cost him a fortune, don't you think? But he can afford it, not like that cheapskate Pádraig."

"I'd better be going." Seth moved quickly toward the door. "I've got some people to see." He paused to take another look at Nanette. "It would take me a year to earn enough to buy a dress like that." He shook his head in a gesture of dismay. Over his shoulder he called back to Miette, "See you Sunday."

After he left, the two women continued to look at each other across the expanse of the dining room.

"Don't your titties get cold?" Miette's tone was sarcastic. "Your nippers must be as hard as rocks in this weather."

Nanette approached her. "Charles Grenough keeps me warm. Who keeps you warm at night and buys you beautiful things? Not that bumpkin who just went out the door, I'd say."

"Why did you come here, Nanette?"

"I've come to offer you a proposition that could be good for both of us."

"Oh, and I thought you might be using that huge tent you call a skirt to sweep the dirt off Montgomery Street."

Nanette acted as if she hadn't heard Miette's sarcasm. "I am serious. It is a very simple way for both of us to make some gold."

Miete gave her an angry look. "I have enough gold. I told you once before I don't want any whore gold, I won't go back to that."

"You don't have to. All I want is to rent one of your private upstairs rooms. That's all."

"What for?"

"What do you think for? So I can entertain gentlemen in private."

"I thought you were Grenough's mistress?"

"Well, I am, of course. That's why I need one of your private rooms. I don't want Charles to know."

"Know what?"

"That I'm entertaining other gentlemen."

"You are a bad woman."

"I have needs, Miette."

"Grenough gave you the gown you're wearing."

Nanette's eyes brightened. "I know. It is beautiful, isn't it? The embroidery on the gold taffeta sets off the color of my eyes so well, don't you think?"

"Didn't you promise to give up entertaining other men?"

"I did, but it's not fair. Charles can't spend all his time with me. He's an important man in the City. I have too much time on my hands. I get bored."

"So you want to have other lovers in secret, is that it?"

"I do. I could have more gold that way. I'd do it discretely, Charles wouldn't know. And that gold would be mine to spend. I wouldn't have to ask him for it. All I need is the use of one of the upstairs rooms. I can come and go through the back door by the kitchen so no one would see me. I need to know the room is available when I need it."

"Every day?"

"Why not? I will pay rent. You would still have other private rooms for your customers to dine in."

Miette thought for a moment. "I suppose you would want to redecorate the room to suit you. You will have to pay me rent and a percentage of what you make... Say twenty-five percent."

"That's an awful lot. Would you consider less?"

"I could, but I won't. I would be taking a risk and need to be compensated for it. If people knew what you were doing up there..."

"Doing up there?" Nanette interrupted. "You think I'm the only one? I'll wager half the men and women using the private rooms are probably naked up there at any given time."

Miette smiled sweetly. "We don't know what they do in the rooms beside having dinner and we don't ask. But we will know what you are doing and that will cost you twenty-five percent."

"Why you little whore."

Miette smiled sweetly again.

Nanette returned the smile. "Think about using one of the upstairs rooms for your own entertaining. I'm sure you could attract a lot of men if you prettied yourself up some. Better than that bumpkin. I could even pass along some of the gentlemen I don't have time for. Think about it, Miette."

The very next morning Miette had another visitor. This one was a slender, pale, blond-haired woman in her thirties wearing a severe black day dress, gloves and a muslin cap, accompanied by a tall Chinese girl barely in her twenties.

"I was told I could find Hannah Runyon here," the woman told Miette in a soft voice.

The Chinese girl stood respectfully just inside the front door, hardly glancing around, her eyes fixed on the floor.

"I am sorry, Madame, Hannah Runyon is no longer here. She has married and left the City."

Their Golden Dreams

The woman seemed crestfallen, defeated. "Oh," she said, "I'm sorry to have troubled you." She continued looking at Miette.

"No trouble, Madame. Is there something I can do for you...?"

"I'm pleased to know Hannah has married," the woman said in a distant voice. "We came to California together. She saved my life in Panama. Did she tell you about that?"

"No, she didn't. I am Miette, Madame, Hannah's partner. I manage the restaurant now since she married a Frenchman and went back to France with him."

The woman brightened. A faint smile crossed her face, adding a bit of life to her dull brown eyes. "How nice for Hannah. How romantic that sounds." She paused, then extended her gloved hand. "I am Caroline Peabody. I was sent to teach at the mission school in Honolulu. I'm just recently returned to San Francisco."

"And this...?" Miette indicated the tall Chinese girl in the doorway. "This is your friend?"

"Oh, yes, excuse me. I got a bit flustered when you said Hannah wasn't here. I was counting on her. God be praised, she nursed me back to health when I contracted cholera crossing the isthmus. This is Li Lan." Caroline Peabody beckoned the girl to come forward. "She was one of my students at the mission school."

Li Lan smiled, but said nothing.

"She speaks English?" Miette asked.

"Oh, yes. She learned at our school. Her father is a sugarcane farmer on Oahu. Her mother died when she was only a child. Her father asked me to bring her with me when I returned to San Francisco hoping she would find a better life here, and perhaps a husband to care for her."

"A better life in San Francisco?" Miette frowned at Caroline Peabody. "That is not something a young Chinese girl is likely to find here."

Li Lan seemed to tremble hearing Miette's words. Her face, which Miette thought very unattractive to begin with, contorted, as if confronted by a demon. She reached out to Caroline Peabody for support.

"I should have known that before I brought her with me, but I had no idea how difficult it is for the Chinese here. It's very dangerous for a Chinese woman in Chinatown without parents I am told. I didn't know. To tell the truth that's why I came looking for Hannah."

"Very dangerous." Miette echoed Caroline Peabody's words. "May I ask what you had in mind for Hannah?"

"May we sit?"

The three women took chairs at one of the tables Miette led them to on the edge of the main dining room. The big room was bathed in morning quiet, as if gathering strength before another busy evening.

"When I brought Lan to San Francisco I thought she would have no trouble finding employment and a place to live in Chinatown. She stayed with me at the mission house near Dupont Street, but almost from the first day she was approached by an older Chinese woman..."

"Ah Daiyu," Li Lan interrupted. "She bad woman."

"She tried to recruit Lan for her...brothel—is that the right word?" Caroline Peabody paused, with a distressed look on her plain-featured face.

Miette nodded sympathetically. "But what was it you wanted Hannah to do?"

"It seems so foolish now... When I learned that Hannah had opened a restaurant here, I thought she might be able to give Lan a job that would keep her away from the evils of Chinatown, and have a more Christian environment."

Their Golden Dreams

"*Mon Dieu!* Even a Christian environment, as you call it, can contain so much evil. I have seen that with my own eyes."

Caroline Peabody stayed silent.

Miette gave her a penetrating look. "I am sorry, Madame, if I have offended you. I grew up in a convent in Paris and there was no Christian spirit there. For the nuns Christianity was like a veil to hide behind."

"I see. Well, I am sorry that I have taken so much of your time." Caroline Peabody rose from the table and motioned to Li Lan to get up. "We will be going now."

Miette rose with them. "I have need of a helper. Does Li Lan have any experience in kitchen work?"

Caroline Peabody stopped her progress toward the door and turned back to face Miette. "She earned her board at our school working in the kitchen."

Miette put her fingers to her lips and thought for a moment. "I see," she said at last. "I could put her to work here, but for now she must stay with you at night. If she is a good worker..."

"I promise work hard," Lan interrupted.

"We'll see about that, Lan. If you are, we might think about fixing up a room for you to live in on our top floor, above the private dining rooms."

Sarafina Bell found Diego in an adobe house on State Street in Santa Barbara where he was renting the back room. It was one of the first homes built in Santa Barbara after the mission days with just two rooms, dirt floors, and a door and two windows for light and ventilation.

"I've been looking for you," she greeted him. "My father wants to talk with you."

"What about, Sarafina?" He gave her an admiring once over and found her slim and dark and pretty in a way he'd never seen her before.

"Please call me Sara, it sounds better." She frowned at him. "He's been hearing that you're speaking out against Americans, stirring up resentment in the town. He wants you to come to the rancho so you two can talk. If you come tonight I'll make supper for us." She looked around at the sparseness of his accommodations shaking her head. "It doesn't look like you get any food here."

"The old Mexicana down the street cooks for me."

"Why are you living like this?"

"I couldn't stay at the ranch, could I? Not with Preston King the new owner."

She came a step closer and reached out to touch his cheek. "What's wrong with you, Diego? You act so angry. The times have changed, even my father calls me Sara now, more American. And they are not so bad as you say. Give them a chance, like I did in Boston."

That evening at sundown they ate a light meal of beef, with beans wrapped in corn tortillas, boiled potatoes and onions in the Bell kitchen. Their conversation stayed mostly about the market in the north for the cattle roaming free in the foothill canyons, and news of Indian raids farther south. It wasn't until they had finished eating that Bell steered the conversation to the real reason for his invitation.

"You've been speaking out against Americans, Diego. We are not your enemies." Before Diego could answer Bell rose from the table and led them onto the veranda, where candles were just beginning to push back on the gathering darkness. Settling himself in a cowhide chair, he drew in a deep breath of evening air, softened with the scent of bay and willow that grew along the nearby stream, and waited for him to respond.

"You're not my enemy, Don Nicholas, but Americans don't get along with us now the way you did before the war, do they? Yankees have no respect for us. We're treated as if we have no rights. We must fight back."

"They do own California now," Sara said. "But you can't blame my father. That's not fair."

"I came with other New Englanders to California in the 1820s—before you and Sara were born," Bell said. "We learned your language. We embraced your religion so we could marry native women and raise families. You can't lay all your troubles at the feet of the Americans."

Diego let his gaze drift to Sara. He saw her intensity in the catch lights from the candles reflected in her large, dark eyes, eyes that were her mother's gift. "In the gold country I saw Americans do unspeakable things—men were hanged from trees without a fair trial, foreign women were abused and raped. Those men who came in search of gold let nothing stand in their way. I despise them for that."

"I'll agree you are right about what has happened here since the gold discovery," Bell said, leaned forward in his chair. "Men hurried to California with only one thought—getting rich. But many are settling here now. They start businesses, buy land in the valleys to farm. They bring their wives and families from back home to start new lives here. They build schools and churches. That is not bad."

"They haven't come down into the south yet." Sara joined the conversation. "Do you expect you can live here in the old ways, Diego?"

Bell shook his head and interrupted. "It won't stay that way for long, Sara. Yes, the Gold Rush divided us—Americans in the north and rancheros here. I think they'll want our land soon enough. Preston King's just one example. More will come."

"I wish I'd never heard his name. Damn him!" Diego slammed a fist into his other palm.

Bell focused on Diego. "I heard at a ranchers' meeting last week the state legislature is considering taxing our land. Did you know that? Some of the legislators in the north think our land here serves no commercial purpose. They would like to see the large ranchos divided into smaller parcels. Then they would encourage more settlers to come. I am told there are powerful men in Sacramento promoting this idea, especially those who support Senator Gwin. If the land tax becomes law I don't think we could stop them."

"That would destroy us."

"It would change the way we live, not destroy us, but we must oppose the proposed law." Bell got up from his chair and started into the casa. "We'll not settle this tonight. Tomorrow I go into town early for another meeting. Some think we should separate from the north, create a new territory and then ask for statehood. I don't know if we could achieve that, but we won't win support for our objectives if you keep picking fights with Yankees."

The sun was down now but the golden afterglow remained in the west. Tall sycamores beside the house became black silhouettes against the sky. Frogs along the stream were beginning their mating calls. Sara and Diego stared into the gathering darkness after Bell left them, each absorbed in their own thoughts.

"A state of our own," Diego echoed, as if he was trying to envision it.

"You would like that?" She stood up and came over to the wooden bench and sat beside him. "We will never live isolated lives on our large ranchos, that time is gone and won't ever come back. You have to accept that."

He felt her warmth when she settled closer to him on the bench. He reached to touch her hand. "Think about it, Sara, all the land from Monterey to San Diego in a new state. We'd still be part of the United States, but we might be free to live the old ways again."

She stayed quiet for several minutes, listening to the evening sounds, staring out beyond the veranda as if she were trying to see what he saw. An almost full moon was rising just above the treetops. It cast a pale light so strong it etched shadows on the adobe walls and added highlights to her dark hair.

Then she looked at him and spoke softly. "I want you to be happy, but you never will be until you give up thoughts like that."

He stood up from the bench. "I must ride back to the pueblo now."

She rose with him but didn't answer. Instead she stood on her toes so she could kiss him on the cheek and put her hand on his shoulder. At first he was startled, but then he didn't resist. They embraced. After another moment their lips found each others.

Nicholas Bell was selected by the other cattlemen to go to Sacramento to represent them at the hearings on the proposed tax. He took Diego and Sara with him in the hope that the spark he had seen between them at the rancho might bloom into romance. He thought it was time they settled down, and a gentle nudge from him would do no harm.

Soon after they disembarked from the coastal steamer in San Francisco, on a windy day in December with a drenching rain falling, Diego went in search of Pádraig Duggan.

"Sure good to see you again," Pádraig greeted him. "I thought our paths might never cross again after the day I saw you off on the steamer."

"You still in politics here, aren't you? I need your advice."

"I am, but things are not going too good for me just now. You might say I'm on thin ice with the Party. Look, I have a meeting with a couple of Party men. Let's have dinner later and talk."

"Can I bring a young woman with me? She's the daughter of the leader of the cattlemen's association in Santa Barbara."

Pádraig gave him a teasing glance. "Sure. A young woman, yer sayin'? A fair lass, I hope. Sweet on her, Diego? Sure, we'll go to *Maison de Paris*, Miette's restaurant—remember her and Hannah? I'll bring Sophie Laughten along."

Maison de Paris was filling up quickly that evening. Couples hurried in the front door anxious to get out of the rain. There was a low buzz of conversations in the dining room punctuated by the orchestra on the second floor balcony, and now and then by the popping of champagne corks. Waiters in formal attire drifted like apparitions between the tables making plates of food appear before the diners as if by magic. When the foursome was assembled, Miette gave Pádraig one of her special greetings and took them to a table in a quiet corner.

"I think I remember you from Angels Camp," she said to Diego as they crossed the restaurant floor.

"I was there two years then went home to Santa Barbara."

"Took all your gold home with you, no? It's nice to have you back. I hope you like *Maison de Paris*."

He grimaced but didn't answer.

She smiled at Sophie and gave Sara an appraising look. "Are you new to the City?"

"I am."

"Welcome then. You're a handsome young woman to be with Diego."

Sara blushed.

Miette handed each of them a menu and left.

Their Golden Dreams

Turning to Sophie, Sara started talking as if they'd always known each other.

"We're going to Sacramento tomorrow, but I wish I could spend more time here. The City seems so exciting. Very different from Boston."

"We don't have many young women in San Francisco," Sophie told her. "At least not proper ones. You'd be a blessing if you stayed here."

When they were settled Diego hardly waited before turning to Pádraig. "The legislature wants a land tax on all the ranchos in the south. Most of the cattlemen would have to sell off parts of their land to pay it. We need to talk to men in Sacramento who can help us."

"I've heard about that. But that's the state's affair. Nothing I can do about it."

"Our whole economy would be ruined," Sara added. "We've got to convince the legislators it's a bad idea. If the land were broken into smaller ranches the cattle might not be able to graze freely."

"I've heard Senator Gwin and Governor Bigler have put their heads together on this. If Gwin really wants something he can usually get the Governor to go along."

"They don't understand how important our land is to our livelihood if they'd break it up."

"I'm a poor one to ask, Diego. The Democrats are very divided now. It looks like I'm on the losing side. Sorry I can't help you. No one would listen."

"You in trouble?"

"These men play for keeps. So far representing the workingmen in San Francisco has kept me safe. But Gwin and his cronies are in control. I got beat up pretty bad once by some of their thugs. Not that I'm scared, but I always have to be on guard. No telling what they might do."

Sophie grabbed his arm. "What's that yer sayin'? Dear God, did I hear ya right?"

"I didn't want to tell you. Don't worry, lass, I'll be all right." He assured her with a gentle pat on her shoulder. "Ya know I can take care of myself."

Sara leaned closer to Sophie and whispered conspiratorially. "Is he your beau?"

"I think so, but sometimes I'm just not sure. He's got a roving eye for a pretty girl."

"He's a fine looking man, Sophie, broad shoulders and strong, handsome face. You'd do well to hold onto him."

"Are you keen on Diego?"

"Funny about that. We played together as children, but now that he's grown I see him in a different way. We're very different. He's shiftless, but I'm very fond of him anyway."

The small orchestra on the balcony began to play for the diners again after a break, but loud voices at the front door competed with the musicians for attention.

Pádraig turned in his seat to look at the source of the voices. "Oh, no," he sighed, "It's Charles Grenough."

"And he's got that trollop on his arm."

Diego shuddered. "I remember her from Pacific House. Made a fool of myself, I did."

"You know her?" Sara's look was more an accusation than a question.

"That whore's been in bed with every man in San Francisco."

Sara looked from face to face and fixed her stare on Diego. "With you?"

Before he could respond, Grenough pushed past Miette and strode toward their table. Nanette trailed behind, gathering up her skirt in her hands to keep it from brushing against the crowded tables. Miette hurried to stay up with them.

With a fierce frown Grenough took a quick look at each face at the table before ignoring them and confronting Pádraig. "You've been talking against us again, Duggan. We've warned you to keep your mouth shut. I thought you'd learned your lesson."

Miette tried to intercede. "Will you be wanting a room upstairs this evening, sir?"

Grenough spun around. "Of course!"

"I won't stop talking to my men. You can't shut me up."

"Who is that man?" Sara whispered to Sophie.

"He and Pádraig don't get along."

"He's very rude."

"For sure he is, but he's a powerful man in the City."

Diego looked from Pádraig to Grenough, trying to avoid Nanette, but saw she was staring straight at him.

The orchestra increased its tempo, playing another waltz.

"One of our private rooms isn't available tonight because it's being redecorated," Miette told Grenough. She shot a quick glance at Nanette.

"Stop interrupting me," he snapped at her. He turned back to Pádraig. "Glad I found you tonight, Duggan. I have a message for you. The Senator wants to see you in his office in the morning. First thing."

The look Nanette gave Miette was withering. "Don't trouble Mister Grenough about that? Surely you can find a room for us."

"Who is that beautiful girl, Sophie?" Sara asked.

"You think she's beautiful? To me she's just a gold-digging Frenchy whore who attaches herself to men like Grenough."

"I'll be there. And I'll tell Senator Gwin the same thing I'm telling you now, Grenough. No slave labor at the diggings while hard-working free men are struggling to make a living. It isn't right."

Nanette put her hand on Miette's shoulder and pulled her back a step. "You little bitch! How could you say that in front of Charles?"

"Well I didn't know if you wanted him in your private room or not."

"Of course I don't want him in there. Are you stupid? He is not to know! When will it be ready?"

"It's painted the way you requested, so now the workers will move the bed and other furniture in tomorrow."

"Well get it done quick, will you?" Nanette lowered her voice to a whisper. "I've a new gentleman I'm anxious to entertain. And find us another room for tonight."

"This is Diego Austen," Pádraig told Grenough. "He represents the cattlemen from Santa Barbara."

Before Grenough could speak, Nanette pushed between Diego and Pádraig. She planted her hands firmly on her hips and gave each of them a disdainful look. "You're certainly two of a kind, a disgusting kind. Neither one of you is worth being called a gentleman. Not like my Charles." She pointed an accusing finger directly at Diego. "That one was so stupid he couldn't even figure out what to do with a beautiful woman like me. The other didn't know how to treat me properly, the way Charles does. You'll never do better than that washed out young Irish seamstress," she said and then turned on Sara. "Who's that skinny girl in the corner? Never seen her before. She looks Mexican. Not a real beauty, I'd say."

"Don't talk like that to my friend. You're nothing but a self-centered whore your own self," Sophie shot back.

"Don't be so hard on her, Sophie. She's just trying to make an impression on our men."

Nanette tittered. "Serves you right. You're just an ignorant Irish seamstress."

"You wouldn't know a gentleman if you tripped over him," Sophie told Nanette. "Not if he was wearing trousers."

"Steer clear of Duggan, he's no good," Grenough warned Diego. "Senator Gwin and the Governor are determined to see California's population grow. All the land south of Monterey is just empty space. Perfect for settlement. Nothing but a few cows wandering around the hills and valleys. It could be fertile farmland. Perhaps a separate state. What we need—"

"Our cattle are putting beef on your dinner tables tonight," Sara interrupted him.

"You're a feisty one aren't you?" Grenough laughed at her. "But that's a joke, young lady. I've had enough of this, Nanette dear. Let's adjourn upstairs. Don't forget, Duggan, be in the Senator's office tomorrow morning."

He started to move away from the table, then he turned back, focusing his hard stare on Sara. "A new state down south might be welcome. War's coming, you know. It's plain as the nose on your face."

"Hope to see you when we come back," Diego told Pádraig as the two met on the sidewalk the next morning. "Sorry about all the fuss last night." December drizzle that threated to turn back into a downpour signaled another dark winter day. Men hurried past them on the sidewalk in both directions, trying to reach their destinations before a new storm broke.

"Not giving up are you?"

"Not at all. We're going up river to Sacramento to talk about the tax."

"Well, I'm off to Senator Gwin's office. Take care of that lass. Hang onto her if ya can, she seems a fine one." He smiled, shook

Diego's hand, turned and headed up the street. It was a quick dash to Gwin's headquarters. Pádraig knew it was important to keep his temper in check, but he was still agitated from last evening's confrontation. He tried to calm himself as he reached the building and shook the rain drops from his jacket and cap. When he walked into the Senator's office and asked to see Charles Grenough, he felt unfriendly faces staring at him.

"What do you want with me? Your meeting's with the Senator," Grenough said without any preliminary pleasantries.

"Can we talk privately?"

"Sure, but make it quick."

Grenough stood by the door signaling him not to sit. Pádraig stood behind a straight-back chair facing him. He wasted no time coming to the point. "My men keep urging me to stand up against this slave labor issue. They think it will take money out of their pockets if it comes about. I can't go against them and don't believe I should."

"You need to change their minds, Duggan. Change your own too. Tell them they're ignorant. Tell them they'll be better off if they just follow the party line. Tell them whatever you want. If you tell them often enough they'll believe it."

"You call it the party line, but not everyone in the Party supports the Senator on this. We're split down the middle."

"Not for long. We've got all the power, not you free-soilers. You and the others got just two choices: get in line or get out of the way. No other choice."

Pádraig gripped the back of the chair tighter. He tried to control his words, but when he spoke again his voice rose, showing his feelings. "So my choice is either I give up everything I believe in or I'll lose my position in the Party, is that it?"

Grenough laughed. "You'll be lucky if it's only your position in the Party you lose. We don't need you anymore, Duggan. We can win without the workingman's vote. Get in line or we'll squash you like a beetle."

Pádraig threw the chair to the side and grabbed Grenough by his coat lapels, pushing him back against the wall. "You scum!" He cocked his fist in Grenough's face. "I've had one too many insults from you."

Grenough was an older man, but he was physically fit. He threw Pádraig's hands off him and pushed back. Then he grabbed him around the waist and started pulling him down.

They wrestled around on the floor, first Grenough on top then Pádraig rolled him off. They rolled into the chair. It slid across the floor and slammed into the wall. When Grenough regained the top again, holding Pádraig on the floor with one hand pressed on his neck, he reached down to his boot with the other and pulled out a knife.

"Stop right now!" A stentorian voice commanded both of them. A pair of hands reached down to pull Pádraig away from Grenough's grasp. "What is going on in here?" the voice demanded.

Pádraig crawled away and got to his feet. Senator William Gwin was standing in front of Grenough glaring. "You two are wrestling around on the floor like savages."

Grenough was trying to return the knife to his boot without being noticed as he got to his feet. "I can no longer suffer this man's insolence. He just attacked me so I defended myself."

"Because you insulted me."

Glaring at Pádraig and still breathing heavily from his exertion, Grenough shouted, "You are a dead man, Duggan! I challenge you to a duel unless you give me an apology."

"Spoken like a true Southern gentleman, which you are not," Pádraig snapped back. "I accept. Arrange the details."

CHAPTER 18

1857

"*I AM RIDING* the trail into the high mountains this morning, Madam. I would be pleased to have you accompany me." Preston King said one bright morning in the new year, sitting astride his horse in the Cañada del Corral courtyard.

"No Señor King, I will not ride with you. Why do you continue to ask me? I have never wanted to ride with you, never wanted any contact with you."

"Madam, this chill between us has no reason to continue. The issue was settled long ago."

"I know that, sir. Yet my anger over what you did to me, and my hostility toward you have not slackened one bit."

King stared down at Delfina. Although still early, the sun promised a hot, dry, breezeless January day ahead. King's horse impatiently pawed the ground, erupting small puffs of dirt as it did. Cawing crows in the nearby oak trees announced the arrival of another rider. Distracted, King turned away to see another horseman coming into the courtyard. "Good morning, Diego," he called out.

Diego just looked at King.

"Have it as you wish. Both of you! I have tried to make your mother's life as comfortable as conditions permit under the circumstances. I have maintained the pretense of a marriage and shared this hacienda with her." He turned in the saddle to give Delfina a piercing stare. "Any other man would have thrown you and Jerome off the land without a second thought to your welfare. I have given you my name and my protection." He gathered the reins and sat erect in the saddle and urged his horse out of the courtyard. Over his shoulder he called back, "Tell the cook I will dine in town this evening." Then he was gone.

Diego dismounted and went to his mother's side. The smile she offered him was faint.

"I don't know how much longer I can endure him. Each day I am reminded that I am a prisoner in my own home."

"What can you do?"

"Only wait. And try to outlive him."

"I don't know how you can share the rancho."

"I keep well apart from him. But enough. Come inside and tell me what brings you out here. I'll tell the maid to get us a pot of tea and we can talk. Perhaps you can cheer me up."

"Where is Jerome?"

"At the corral with the vaqueros. Doing all the things you used to do at his age."

The air inside the hacienda still held early morning coolness. Diego followed his mother into the sala where the sunlight was streaming in the window, illuminating dust motes that floated around the curtains. They sat facing each other, Delfina on the loveseat, Diego in a cushioned chair across a low table from her. After a few minutes the kitchen girl delivered the pot of tea and cups.

"I do have some news to tell you," he started.

"Good news, I hope. We've been without much good news since the war ended."

"The ranchers want to elect me to the state legislature."

She was brought up short. "You, Diego? Why you? Would that be a good thing?"

"For a couple of reasons. I guess the first is that I've been speaking out that we need to be better represented in Sacramento. The men think the current assemblyman isn't forceful enough in pursuing our interests. The other reason is that when I went up to San Francisco and the Capitol with Don Nicholas and Sara, I met a lot of men from the southern part of the state. They encouraged me to become more active. The ranchers here agree. So my name will be put forward in the next election. In fact, I'm going back north tomorrow on the steamer."

She was thoughtful. "We need better men representing us, that's true. I remember when you stood up to Captain Frémont during the war. It was a brave thing to do."

"You have always been an example of bravery to me. You and my father. Ever since Will Thornton sailed off and left you alone, you have been the bravest person I know."

Without thinking she reached out and touched the carved jade horses on the table between them. She gave a little sigh. "A long time ago."

"It was ten years. I didn't know then—Victoriano told me. He said you were very brave to let Thornton leave without telling him about the baby."

"Brave? Perhaps. I didn't want to hold him back. He needed to return to Boston."

"Did you love him, Mother?"

"I did."

"More than my father?"

"Not more, but different. I loved each of them differently." She hesitated a moment, lost in a private memory. Then a smile parted her lips and put a sparkle in her eyes. "How strange it is that the two men I have loved in my life have been Americans."

"When I was panning gold in Angels Camp a woman I met mentioned Will Thornton's name."

Delfina didn't speak for several moments. Then she asked, "How did she know him?"

"Her name was Hannah Runyon. She said she was his daughter, but never knew him directly." Diego stopped speaking and watch his mother's reaction. Her face stayed blank. "Hannah would be Jerome's sister, wouldn't she?"

"Half sister."

He could see his mother was lost in thought.

"She said she had never known her father."

"This woman was in Angels Camp you say?"

"Yes, but she had come there from Boston. She told me Will Thornton had left her mother—an Irish woman—on the wharf when he sailed off for California."

"I'm not surprised. He was a restless, ambitious man. Still, I loved him."

"I have not always been a good son to you, but I have always loved and respected you. I have some other news to tell you. Sarafina Bell and I are going to marry."

Delfina's face broadened into a happy smile showing her teeth and the fullness of her cheeks. Her eyes sparkled as she reached across the table to touch his hand. "That is fine news, very fine news, son. I have watched you two together over the last few months and I've seen affection between you grow."

There was another pause in the conversation, as her thoughts seemed to slip back to a past time. The dust motes had stopped dancing by now as the sun rose above the house, but the coolness remained. Diego waited for Delfina to come back to him. Reaching out he let his fingers trace the shape of the jade horses on their ebony stand on the table. They were a mare and stallion carved in China that had grazed on the table in the sala as long as he could remember.

"Promise me you will treat Sara with respect. Treasure her."

Abruptly, as if she'd just thought of something, Delfina rose from the love seat, dabbing a tear from the corner of her eye as she did. She went out to the casita she and Jerome had moved to when Preston King took over the rancho. After searching there for a few minutes she returned and resumed her place.

"I have a very special gift for you and Sara. I have been saving it for you since you were born." As she spoke she unwrapped a cloth. Inside the cloth was a small, fragile basket. "This is a Chumash seed basket. I want you to have it and to pass it on to your children and their children. Your grandmother's mother wove it a long time ago while she was waiting for your grandmother, Cayatu, to be born. She told Cayatu the basket contained the life stories of her Chumash family. I am very proud of my Chumash blood, Diego, and I want you to be, too. As long as the basket passes from generation to generation in our family our bloodline will be strong regardless of any adversities we face. It is where our bravery comes from."

Later that afternoon, after Diego had left with the seed basket carefully placed in his saddlebag, Preston King returned. Delfina saw him from the sala window, slumped over the saddle horn. She was reluctant to go out to see what might be wrong because she couldn't stand to be near him. But when King still hadn't dismounted a few minutes later she went onto the veranda. Standing there, she called in a loud voice, "If you've been drinking whisky again I'm not going to help you."

"Not drinking," he replied in a weak voice.

"What then?"

"Snake bite."

Their Golden Dreams

She paused a moment. "How long ago?"

"Maybe an hour."

"Up on the trail?"

"Yes."

Reluctantly, she stepped off the veranda and moved closer to him. "How?"

"Got off the horse. Young rattler by a rock. Side of the trail. Didn't see him. Having trouble getting my breath. My heart is pounding."

"Where'd he bite you?"

"Leg. Above my boot."

"Did you get the venom out?"

"No."

She gasped. "You are a fool, Señor King. You have to act quickly when a rattlesnake bites. You shouldn't ride alone if you don't know what to do."

"Seems like you're asking an awful lot of questions. Shouldn't you take me to a doctor?"

She looked him over, assessing his condition. "Doctor is in town ten miles away. From the looks of you, you wouldn't survive the carriage ride. Besides, there's nothing a doctor could do for you at this point."

"So I am going to die?"

"Sounds like the venom's spread throughout your body if your heart's pounding. I'll help you into the casa. You can lie down. Yes, I think you will die, but you might try praying if you have a God."

He all but fell off the horse into her arms. She shuddered at the feel of him, but helped him into the hacienda and told him to lie down on his bed.

"Don't let me die," he begged. She spread a blanket over him to ease his shaking from the chills that wracked his body.

"I can't help you. There is nothing anyone can do. You were a fool to act so stupidly, riding into the high mountains alone..."

"I asked you to come with me," he interrupted.

"...without any protection. Young rattlesnakes are the worst, they can't control the amount of venom they eject. You're not cut out for this life, Señor King. You don't know things you need to know to survive on a rancho like this."

King's eyes were glazing over. He trembled more weakly than before. He looked at her with what might have been a weak smile. She couldn't tell.

"You don't care if I die."

She turned away, uncomfortable with the words forming on her lips. Her eyes scanned around the room she had not been in since he took over the rancho. There were only clothing and a few other things on a corner shelf. Her eyes settled on a strange leather object she couldn't identify so she took it down from the shelf to inspect it. Staring at it for just that moment it came to her with a suddenness that sent her reeling. Her breathing stopped. The anger she felt contorted her face. Diego's name was scratched into the leather. She felt dizzy and had to reach out to the wall to steady herself. *Dios en el cielo me ayude* she prayed to herself. She was holding the money belt.

She went to the bed, still holding it, and glared down at King. "Your are an evil man, Señor King. A horrible, evil man! You stole my rancho and then paid for it with Diego's gold. You are beyond all redemption. You will die and burn in Hell. I hope it is a long, painful death so you suffer." She turned and walked out of the room.

Fog was retreating over the sand hills toward the Pacific in San Francisco when Diego found Pádraig eating breakfast at the What Cheer Café. Pádraig sat alone wearing his best frock coat, with his top hat on the chair beside him. He picked it up to make room for Diego.

"I wish I could be as calm as you are." Diego slipped into the chair. "I didn't sleep last night."

Pádraig offered his hand in greeting and a warm smile. "Sorry to put you to this, my friend. It'll all be over soon. I'm glad you could come back to San Francisco. At least we'll have a dry day for the duel."

"I am proud to be your second. But how has it comes to this?"

"I guess I brought it on myself, but it's been getting worse for awhile now. Someone had to stand up to the Chivs. Me, I guess."

He picked up his spoon and resumed eating the oatmeal mush from the steaming bowl in front of him. Beside it on the table were a plate of buckwheat pancakes and a dish of stewed prunes. He washed the oatmeal down with hot coffee from a tin mug.

He put the mug down. "There's something I must tell you."

Diego picked at a sourdough roll on the table.

"I am going to die today."

"No you're not. You'll be—"

"Just listen to me now and keep quiet. I am going to die today because I am not going to fire my pistol at Grenough."

Diego's stomach churned. He started to speak and then stopped and stared at his friend.

"I am not going to aim at Grenough," he said again. "I will fire into the air."

"By God, Pádraig, you accepted his challenge. You have to fight!"

"I don't. I couldn't ignore his challenge now could I? I was the one who started the wrestling match. But I don't have to kill

Grenough. If he kills me that is my fate."

He took a final sip from the mug, then took in a breath. "We were dead poor in Ireland in '44 when my father sent me away. There wasn't enough food in our house to go around. I lived on the street, mostly begging and sometimes stealing. One evening I was in an alley in Dublin eating a crust of bread I'd found behind a pub. Another guy saw me, a poor old man in worse shape that I was. He tried to take that crust away from me. We fought over it. In my panic to hang on to the crust I picked up a rock and hit him in the head. I killed him. The crust we had fought over was in crumbs and little use to either of us by then. I was sick at the sight of the man's crushed skull. Vomited all over. I can never get rid of that memory. I won't kill again."

Diego could see the anguish in his eyes. He stayed quiet listening.

When Pádraig finished he went silent. There was nothing more he could say. He took the napkin that was tucked in his waistcoat like a bib, folded it and set it down at the edge of the table. He gave his friend a grin. "Okay, let's get on with this."

There was a small gathering on the grassy peninsula that jutted into Lake Merced, almost cutting it in half. The light fog hovering just offshore, still cast a gauze net over the scene when Diego and Pádraig arrived. A few carriages were parked under trees well to the rear of the dueling area. Saddle horses grazed untied nearby. Unsure what his responsibilities were as a second, as soon as he dismounted Diego walked toward the group of men surrounding Charles Grenough. They made way for him as he approached. Grenough extended his hand.

"I was wondering if your man was going to show up or not. It was getting late."

Diego looked steadily at Grenough with an expressionless face. He gave an exaggerated shrug. "Mister Duggan stayed to finish his breakfast. It was a large one."

Their Golden Dreams

Grenough's second urged his man to the rear and confronted Diego, holding out a wooden box with an open lid. Twin dueling pistols nestled inside on a bed of red velvet. They were old, single shot flintlock pistols, with highly polished walnut handles inlaid with silver. The man pushed the pistol case toward him.

"These are very special dueling pistols. Senator William Gwin has lent them for this occasion. They came with him from Mississippi. He is not here, of course, but he sends the message that he hopes this matter can be settled quickly and with honor in a gentlemanly fashion. Both pistols are loaded. You may inspect them and select one."

Grenough pushed forward again. "Look, I was wronged by Duggan, but I'm a reasonable man. If he offers me a sincere apology we can end this right now."

Diego studied Grenough's face. It held a smile, but the look in his eyes told a different story. They were fanatical eyes.

"I will certainly extend your offer, sir."

With no more talk Diego selected a pistol. He felt the smoothness of the grip and put his finger lightly against the trigger. He held the barrel close to his nose. The smell of the light coating of oil was not offensive. Then he bowed slightly and walked back to Pádraig, who was now surrounded by a crowd of men, mostly the firemen, dockworkers and other San Francisco workingmen he championed. When he explained Grenough's offer, the group pleaded with Pádraig to accept it.

Sophie Laughten, her face drawn and paler than usual, had come with her mother and now leaned on Emma for support. She wasn't crying, but had been, and showed clear signs she might start again any minute. They had been standing just off to the side of the knot of men, but now she rushed forward. "You must accept," she cried out. "Please!"

"Yes, apologize." Miette, who had come with Seth, added. "Charles Grenough is an unprincipled man who probably means to kill you if you go ahead with the duel. I've seen it happen in France."

"I will not apologize to anyone in this carpet-bagging band of southerners who are trying to steal California. I would rather die here today than do that."

Sophie wobbled a few steps as if she might faint. Tears began anew when she heard his words. Miette let out a groan and huddled close to Seth who put a protective arm around her. Others in the somber crowd urged Pádraig to reconsider. He shook his head, emphatically rejecting their pleas. He took the pistol Diego handed him without inspecting it. Smiling, bowing slightly to the crowd, he turned and walked toward the referee. The people who had gathered around him grew quiet. At the last minute he turned back and walked to where Sophie stood. He held her by her shoulders at arms length and looked into her face. "Please do not cry for me," he said.

As Diego followed to where the referee waited, he saw Nanette in the band of people with Grenough. She stood proudly beside him, clutching his arm, wearing one of her finest gowns. Her hooped skirt blossomed out from her waist, reminding him of a church bell. She posed there, as if the crowd had come to honor her. The look on her face was one of girlish excitement. She ignored Diego. The gravity of what was about to take place pushed down on him. He took a deep breath and stood behind Pádraig, silently praying for his friend.

The grassy plain along the lakeshore grew so quiet, the crowd of spectators could hear the referee's instructions. Each pistol contained only one ball. After each was fired the duel would be ended regardless of the outcome. Glaring at each other, both men nodded their understanding. Then they turned to stand back to back. At the command they began counting off steps. Time stopped as they paced away from each other.

Diego watched for any sign of fear in Pádraig. He saw none. Miette clung to Seth's right arm. Sophie stood with Emma, her face buried in her mother's bosom unable to watch, but peeking out every few seconds nevertheless.

When Pádraig and Grenough had paced off ten steps they stopped, waiting for the referee's next command. When he gave it they turned to face each other, their pistols still aimed skyward.

"Noooo..." It was a long, low, pathetic moan, more animal than human that came from deep in Sophie's throat. It sliced the silence like a razor, unsettling the spectators, causing them to look away, but thrilled by it at the same time. Even the duelists gave quick, sideways glances.

And then the final command came from the referee. "You may fire at will gentlemen."

Charles Grenough lowered his pistol to aim it at Pádraig who stared straight ahead at him. Then, his own pistol still raised over his head, Pádraig pulled the trigger and fired into the air. The shot made an inconsequential popping sound that hardly disturbed the stillness of the scene. Pádraig lowered the weapon to his side and waited.

Grenough looked at him in disbelief. Sophie Laughten screamed and fainted on the ground. Diego bit sharply into his lower lip to keep his emotions in check, but inwardly he screamed along with Sophie. He looked at Grenough and saw a faint smile grow on his face. A collective gasp rippled through the watchers on both sides of the field. Nanette's face held an excited, almost maniacal, expression. Pádraig did not move. He stood tall, facing Grenough, unblinking.

Grenough hardly paused. He extended his arm. His face still held the smile. It creased the corners of his mouth and seemed to light up his eyes. At the last moment Nanette rushed up to stand beside him, her hooped skirt brushing his leg as he pulled the trigger.

Pádraig fell. Spectators on both sides screamed. Looking at one another for reassurance, they found none on the faces of their friends. Many of them turned their backs.

Some of the men who had come to support Pádraig started toward him, but Diego waved them back. He ran to his friend. Pádraig's white shirt was stained red. In the next instant, Sophie was on her knees beside him, sobbing through her tears.

"I'll be all right," he said, trying to rise up. "The ball hit my shoulder, knocked me off my feet, but I'm all right." He gave a little chuckle. "Nanette must have upset Grenough's aim. That little ball packed one heck of a wallop, I can tell you." He smiled. His trembling hand reached out to take Sophie's.

Lifting her skirt, she tore a long piece of fabric from the hem of her petticoat. She used it to stop the blood pulsing from his wound. With the gentlest of touches she wound the fabric into a bandage around his shoulder. Miette joined them and looked down. When she saw that Pádraig was alive she knelt to hug him carefully.

"*Je remercie Dieu.*"

Others gathered around them now. Sophie began giving directions to the men coming forward. "He is coming home with me," she commanded. "Carry him to our carriage. We'll take him to the shop. I'll summon the doctor there."

Diego looked across the field where Nanette was hugging Grenough then he turned away.

CHAPTER 19

1857

IT WAS MORE than a week later when Nanette charged into *Maison de Paris* in the middle of the morning. "My boudoir is finally ready?" She asked. "It has taken you long enough."

"It was you who kept changing your mind about how you wanted it decorated. I'm sorry now I agreed to rent it to you."

"Oh, hush! I'm paying you well enough. Did you hang the pink curtain over the window?"

"It's done!"

The women exchanged looks that were far from friendly.

"Don't go back on your word, Miette. I've got big plans." Nanette hesitated with pursed lips before continuing. "Remember the bumpkin who was here the day I came by?"

Miette stiffened. "Seth?"

"Yes, that's the one. I can tell you he is not worth going after. You should get rid of him."

"How do you know that?"

"I saw him a few days after the duel. I invited him to buy me a glass of champagne at City Hotel."

"You did what?"

"Nothing much happened. I teased him for a while, but when I mentioned my price he got very squirrelly. Made all sorts of excuses that he had to get back to work. I could see he didn't have any gold."

"How could you do that? Do you ever think of anyone but yourself?"

"Don't be so silly. I was just having some fun with him. And look how I've saved you from wasting your time. You should be thanking me."

"You are a bad woman, Nanette. A very bad woman. Some day you will pay for all your evil deeds."

"Aren't you a righteous whore these days."

"Go away! We have a business arrangement and that's all. So if you don't pay on time, I'll throw you out."

"You're the nicest girl I've ever known," Seth told Miette one evening. It was the first time he had been bold enough to steal a kiss.

"There are things about me you don't know. I should tell you, but if I do you won't think so highly of me."

"Nothing you could say would change how I feel about you."

"Don't be so sure."

"That other girl—Nanette—told me about your life in Paris. It doesn't matter to me."

"She told you?"

"It doesn't matter. What's important is us being together now. The people who come to dine at *Maison de Paris* know how kind and sweet you are. You take care of everyone. I'm proud to be seen with you. In San Francisco no one pays any attention to the past."

Miette was speechless. "You know about my past life? Nanette told you?"

"I know."

Not long afterward, as diners were coming into *Maison de Paris* in a steady stream, Miette was startled to see Charles Grenough coming in the door with a woman on his arm. It was not Nanette.

Their Golden Dreams

"Come now, I can't wait in line all night. We need a private dining room," he told Miette, pushing his way to the front of the line and pulling the pretty young woman along with him.

Miette had never seen the girl before. "Certainly, sir. It's good to have you with us again tonight." She looked down at her list. "Have you reserved a room?"

"I always have an upstairs room when I come for dinner. Certainly you won't let me down tonight."

"I'm afraid we are completely filled."

"Nonsense. I am Charles Grenough, Senator Gwin's assistant. I know you can find us a private room on your second floor."

Miette thought for a moment, then looked back again at Grenough and the woman. A pleasant smile lighted her face. "Certainly, sir. I think we can accommodate you and the lady. Right this way. Please follow me." She led Grenough and the young woman across the main room toward the stairs. "Is this your daughter?" she asked Grenough as sweetly as she could.

He didn't answer. His look said she was not.

The orchestra was tuning its instruments. The main room was filling up with men in formal attire and beautifully dressed women chatting together in low voices.

"I don't think I've seen you in here before, she said in a hushed voice over the low hum of conversation and clink of glasses, turning to the girl as they crossed the restaurant. "New to the City?"

"Oh yes." The girl was effusive, with just a trace of giggle in her voice. "I came in on the Pacific Mail two days ago. I went to the government office looking for help and met Mister Grenough. He's been so helpful. And now he's taking me to dinner."

Miette started up the stairs. At the top she smiled at the orchestra playing a slow waltz, and gave a questioning look at the waiter who was always posted there. He nodded to her almost imperceptibly. She returned the nod then stepped over to one of the private room doors and put her hand on the doorknob.

"I think this room will best suit your needs tonight," she told Grenough. "It's been redecorated."

With that she opened the door wide. Grenough and the girl were treated to a lavishly decorated room with paintings in gilt frames on the walls, mahogany furniture, a plush red carpet, pink curtains at the window and a large canopied bed. Clothed only in corset and pantalets, Nanette lay there with a man in his long johns beside her. Miette stepped back so Grenough and the girl had a clear view.

In Épernay, Hannah had just finished dressing her toddler when Madame Benard's maid knocked on her door.

"Madame wishes to see you in the smoking room," she told her.

The smoking room was in the main wing of the mansion, just to the left of the entrance, vestibule and grand gallery. Achille Benard senior had used it as a gentlemen's room for after dinner brandy and cigars. In fact, it was often the room where foreign buyers and Achille conducted business, Luc had told her. But now Luc used the room as a private study. To the seventeenth century furniture and the art and tapestries that graced the walls, he had added an eighteenth century mahogany and bronze gilt writing table where he liked to read and answer his correspondence each morning. Hannah's mother-in-law was seated at the table now.

She told Hannah to shut the door and pointed her to sit in a carved giltwood armchair near the fireplace that did its best to take the January chill off the room. Hannah had felt intimidated the few times she'd been in the room before because of the age and grandeur of the furnishings. She wondered now, if that was the reason her mother-in-law chose it for this conversation.

More likely, she decided, Madame Benard had chosen it because the old woman liked to usurp Luc's place when he was traveling.

There were few pleasantries exchanged between the two women. Madame Benard wasted no words.

"Your child is a great inconvenience to me. I deplore the way you have insinuated yourself into my son's life and now try to establish a place in our proud family by having a male child. I can see past your naming him for my late husband. It is just one more of your wily tricks. Women like you have always been after other people's fortunes."

Hannah was not altogether unprepared for her mother-in-law's antagonism. It had been a continuing struggle between them for the past two years, but the force of the old lady's outburst today overwhelmed her. She felt as if she were shrinking down into her chair. Short of breath, as if she'd taken a physical blow to her stomach, she stared at her adversary for several moments, then regained her composure. She didn't want to strike back at Luc's mother, but she knew she had to for his sake and the sake of their son.

"It is unfortunate you have chosen not to like me, Madame Benard. In the beginning I thought we could be civil with each other because we shared a love for your son. But it is your choice to dislike me and that saddens me."

"How could I like you?" the woman interrupted. "You are not one of us! And never can be."

"But I am your son's wife. I share his bed. I've given him a son of his own. You can never change that. You cannot compete with me for his affection. You will lose. If you continue to oppose me you will only wind up a lonely old woman."

"I will never accept you or your son into the House of Benard. I tell you this now, while Luc is traveling in America, so that you can pack your belongings and leave, taking the child with you.

I will pay your passage back to California if you agree never to contact Luc again. He and I will manage our business together. There is no place for you here! Do you hear me?"

The feeling Hannah had as she sat facing the old woman was familiar. Madame Benard was going to take Luc away from her. She would be alone again to raise her son on her own. How could it ever be different?

She sat there in silence. The old feeling she hadn't had since Luc had come into her life returned, like a stray dog. So consumed by her feelings of rejection, she did not hear the soft knocking at the smoking room door.

"Who is there? Go away!" the old woman's voice called out.

"It is Camille André. It is important I speak with you and the young Madame Benard."

"Enter then. But be quick with whatever it is."

Rather timidly, André opened the door. He looked at the two stone-faced women staring at him. His own look said he didn't want to be there.

"What is it? Problems with production? You must keep up with the orders Luc sends back to us from New York and Boston."

"No Madame, there are no problems with our production." André's face was ashen. "It is Luc," he said in a trembling voice. He hesitated, shifting from one foot to the other before speaking again. "Luc is dead, Madame. He died when a train and his carriage collided in New Jersey. We just received word from America. They have shipped us his body."

Weeping, Hannah dressed for the funeral days later. Little Achille clung to her skirts, more confused and frightened by his mother's tears than the grief he was too young to comprehend. There had been no time to have a mourning dress made so she wore one of her plain dresses her maid had dyed black, with long sleeves and a high collar. Tying the black bonnet under her chin and lowering the veil to cover her face, she took the little boy's hand.

"Come now," she told him. "It is time."

The carriages were waiting in the courtyard, lined up behind the hearse. Snow from a light sprinkling the evening before covered the ground. The workmen waited behind the carriages, talking to one another in low, respectful voices and blowing on their hands to keep warm. They fell silent as the casket was brought out from the underground cave where it had rested since its arrival and loaded into the hearse.

Hannah started toward the lead carriage whose matched black horses snorted and pawed the ground impatiently, their steamy breath visible in the cold air. She stopped short when she saw Luc's mother had usurped her rightful place. Turning away, she lifted up her son and took a seat in the second carriage.

At a somber pace the procession moved off down the hill to the village church in the center of Épernay. Led by Camille André, hats in hand, wearing black armbands on their sleeves, the men walked behind the carriages.

Inside the dim church, stone-gray to match the afternoon outside and her mood, Hannah saw Madame Benard had taken her seat in the front pew. It didn't matter to her anymore, she thought, as she took a seat in the pew in the next row. Better to say her goodbyes to the only man she had ever loved, and contemplate her future alone, with only her son, Luc's son, beside her, she decided.

And what was that future to be? Hannah knew what Luc had wanted for her. But how could she survive in this land of strange customs in a house where she was not wanted? What was better: to return to a comfortable life in San Francisco or abide by her late husband's wishes? Why not take the part of Luc left to her and leave the conflict behind?

Luc was buried alongside his father in the graveyard in back of the church. Hannah listened to the priest intone the Latin words, trying to calm Achille's fidgeting. When the priest finished speaking, she startled Madame Benard and the others by taking the boy by the hand and approaching the grave. Speaking a few words to him no one else could hear, she knelt on the ground with the boy. Lifting her veil, she leaned forward and kissed the coffin lightly. Then she rose and walked to her carriage, holding Achille's hand, keeping her tear-filled eyes focused straight ahead.

Back at the mansion, Madame Benard hurried inside for warmth. Hannah remained in the yard, thanking the men for their devotion to her husband and accepting their humbly spoken condolences. When they had dispersed only Camille André remained.

"What will you do now, Madame?" he asked in a gentle voice.

"Oh, Camille," she sighed heavily, "I am not sure what to do."

"Will you go back to America now?"

"It would be easier but perhaps not best."

"No one would fault you for going back."

"I suppose not."

"Walk this way with me, Madame." André led her inside the winery building where they were out of sight of the mansion. Standing beside the stacks of wine barrels he asked her, "Do you know what will happen if you leave us?"

Hannah didn't reply.

"The *House of Benard et fils* will fail. The old woman will try to do everything her way."

"Is it such a bad way?"

"It is. Luc saw that when he brought you to Épernay. She is wedded to the old ways. She doesn't listen. She wants to keep making sweet champagne. What old Achille sent to San Francisco was much better."

"What can I do?"

"Stay. Take over the champagne business."

Hannah laughed. "Me? You have tried to teach me, but I still know little about the business."

"Luc told me you knew little about managing a restaurant but you learned."

"I had a lot of help in San Francisco, including Luc's."

"I will help you, Madame. The two of us can build a great champagne house. That is what Luc saw. What he wanted. It would be your son's birthright."

She looked out the lone window and let her eyes roam around the courtyard and then over the snow-covered vines in the valley far across the river. In the two years she had lived here with Luc she had tried to make it feel like a home. But it wasn't, it belonged to Luc's mother.

"I don't know, Camille. I want to stay. There is nothing much for me back in California. I'd like to build the business with your help that Achille could inherit. But we both know my mother-in-law will try to control the business as she tries to control me. What would be different?"

"Indeed she will try. But the future is up to you. You are the only one with the power to stop her."

"Oh, Camille, what power? How could I do that?"

"You can. You know that Luc went to his *notaire* to draw up a will. He showed it to me before asking me to put it in the safe." Camille took a large envelope from inside his jacket pocket and handed it to her. "You should read it."

"It is only paper, Camille. Paper or not, it would take a strong resolve to battle with Luc's mother each day."

"The paper can give you that resolve."

"I cannot read French. Will you help me?"

André smiled. "Certainly."

Hannah reached out to take the envelope. She rested her other hand on his shoulder, something it would have been improper to do before.

"How can I thank you for being my friend? For everything you have done for Luc and me." She looked at him and smiled. In his eyes she could see what a good and honest man he was. But she thought what he was suggesting might be the most difficult request anyone had ever made of her. He was offering a challenge and a promise at the same time. "Can we meet privately this afternoon?"

The winter's darkness descended early in Épernay. Oil lamps did their best to light the mansion and dissipate the gloom. Fireplaces had been lighted in most of the rooms, but a chill still lingered in the air when Hannah tapped on Madame Benard's boudoir door. Entering the room she was overwhelmed by the dazzle of gold and crystal and marble that met her eye. The old lady sat in a heavily upholstered Louis XV armchair near the fireplace in her dressing gown, a blanket wrapped around her, glaring.

"I suppose you have come to tell me when you and the boy will depart," she greeted Hannah.

Hannah summoned the best smile her face could manage, but it was weak and lacked sincerity. "No, Madame. I have come to tell you I have decided to let you live out your life in this house. With some changes in your accommodations of course."

"How dare you speak that way to me?"

"I think you know how I dare. This mansion and the champagne house, belong to me and my son now."

She could see the start of panic in her mother-in-law's face, but the old woman kept her voice tightly under control. "I will never let that happen." The words left her mouth like gunshots. "I will fight you to the end."

"You will fight a losing battle. I will have French law on my side."

"What law? I am the Madame Benard. The house belongs to me. It was my husband's."

Hannah took a deep breath and hoped the old woman hadn't noticed her slight hesitation. "No," she said, "I am Madame Benard now. The House of Benard, this mansion and everything in it belong to me and Achille now. It is all here in Luc's will. And it is French law that the son inherits from his father, as you know."

The old woman stared at her dumbstruck. She looked at the papers Hannah handed to her as if they were knives pointed at her breast, and refused to take them. "My own son," was all she could say.

"Your own son," Hannah repeated. "I think he saw the meanness in you. He had seen it even when he was a young boy. He saw the mean-spirited way you treated his father and all the workers. He wanted to put a stop to it."

Still standing and holding the papers, Hannah looked down on the woman with an expression that might have been one of pity. "I will be clear," she said. "You can live out your life under the roof of my house—with some changes in your living quarters naturally—or we will pack your personal belongings and put them out on the street, and you along with them. That is the choice you must make now. It is the consequence of how you have lived."

"You cannot do this to me," the old woman stammered. "I am the widow Benard."

"No longer, Madame" Hannah said, smiling. "Now I am the Widow Benard."

CHAPTER 20

1860

WHEN HANNAH ARRIVED back in San Francisco after a five-year absence, she walked directly to *Maison de Paris*. Miette stopped what she was doing at the front desk and stared slack-jawed at her. The look on her face was hard for Hannah to read. There was joy reflected in her dark eyes at their reunion, but they also held a hint of apprehension.

"I thought I would never see you again," Miette stammered. Pulling herself together, she took a couple of tentative steps toward Hannah. "Have you come back to stay?"

In an instant Hannah understood the implication of Miette's question. "Oh, no." She laughed, then hurried across the threshold to embrace her friend. "I've just come for a visit. I couldn't wait to see you and the restaurant again." After they hugged, she added, "I was hoping to arrange a small dinner for some of our old friends."

"Of course." Relieved now Miette's tone lightened. " How about this evening? I'll send out a messenger to round them up and I'll have the chef make a special dish." She stood back to inspect Hannah. "Don't you look the prosperous bourgeois French Madame? Everyone will be glad to see you again."

Hannah let her eyes scan the restaurant.

"What do you think?" Miette gestured to the large dining room with a wave of her hand. "Since you left I have worked hard to maintain the high standards you and Luc set when we opened."

"It looks as wonderful as the day we left. And you, my dear, are just as pretty as I remember. You haven't aged one bit."

"But I am forgetting my manners." She smiled and her dark eyelashes fluttered with excitement. "We must have a long chat."

"I have a son, Achilles. He's four now. Born shortly after we settled in Épernay."

Miette had a knowing look. "So it was a romantic journey for you two."

A bittersweet smile crossed Hannah's face, but then she turned serious again. "Luc died before Achille turned two. Did you know? Killed in an accident in New Jersey."

"I did not. I am very saddened to hear that. Let's not stand about like two strangers. I can see we have very much to talk about. We'll go up to my room where we can be comfortable and talk." Miette led the way to a second floor room where they settled into comfortable deeply cushioned armchairs.

"Wasn't this a private dining room?" Hannah looked around the room at the plush furnishings that included a large canopied bed.

"It was. Some of the furniture is left over from when I rented it to a customer. I use it now as my room so I am always close to the restaurant. Did you see how San Francisco has changed since you left? There is not so much interest in private dining rooms now."

"I saw the City was changed as the steamer landed. It docked at a new place. The cove has disappeared."

"Filled in to make land for new businesses. There are fine new homes—large homes—built on the hills now. Most of the southern men who entertained privately are gone. Run out of town, they were. Everyone thinks we are close to war. Do they talk of that in France? Many of the men returned to their homes in the South to avoid being arrested here. Pádraig says he will go east to fight if war starts."

Miette reached behind her chair to pull on a call rope. "Let's have tea while we talk. Tell me about your life in France. Strange, isn't it, the American woman has gone to France and the Parisian girl is here in San Francisco."

"I will tell you—there is much to tell—but first I want you to know I am going to see an attorney while I am here. I will sign over to you all my interest in *Maison de Paris*."

The joyous look coming over Miette's face went far beyond gratitude. It was a look of wonderment, with perhaps a touch of disbelief. "You would do that for me?" Her voice was suddenly choked.

"I could do no less for you. And I should have done it sooner. Without you at my side as my companion none of the good things would ever have happened."

"Ah but, *mon cher*, you are the one who changed the course of my life. I was selling myself on the streets of Paris in order to eat. I was worthless. But you believed in me enough in Angels Camp to take me out of the gambling hall and put me to work."

"It was you who convinced me."

They looked at each other with deep affection. Then they arose and embraced each other again. The door opened and a tall Chinese girl came into the room.

"Please bring us a pot of tea and two cups, Lan. Perhaps a slice of berry pie for each of us, too. We are celebrating. This is the fine woman I've told you about who started the restaurant."

The Chinese girl bowed. Then she backed out of the room.

"How is your life in Épernay?"

Their Golden Dreams

"It is a good one. I will never return to the United States to live. The House of Benard belongs to me now, since Luc's death, and I will pass it on to Achille when he is grown. My mother-in-law, Luc's mother, died last year. She was a troublesome old woman. We did not get along. When I stepped into Luc's shoes I had to push her aside. I've learned much about the business from Camille, my *Chef de Cave*. Together we are making the finest champagne in France. Our business grows steadily. Achille and I live alone in the large mansion. We have servants who look after all our needs. It's like a fairy tale, Miette, but I miss Luc very much. And I do get bored in Épernay so I am thinking of having a house in Paris too. Perhaps one day you will come visit me there." Hannah stopped to look wistfully at Miette. "Our lives have crisscrossed, but we have both been fortunate. Is there a man in your life now, Miette?"

"No one permanent. I've had lovers since you've been away, but no man wants to raise a family with a woman who has a past like mine. I understand that. There was one who said my past didn't matter to him, but in the end it did matter. Many young women have come to San Francisco since you left so he was able to find a wife with a better past." She laughed sardonically. "I am very concerned about the plight of young Chinese women in the City. Your friend Caroline Peabody brought Li Lan to me several years ago. Ever since then I have committed myself to rescuing young girls who are forced into prostitution in Chinatown. Many of those girls who become sex slaves die of starvation or disease. It is an intolerable situation. Saving as many of them as I can has become very important to me. And I have many friends now, some of the most important men in the City. I am accepted as a community leader. They include me in civic matters and escort me to social events where I am very popular, and it doesn't hurt that I still have my good looks. So, my life is like yours, perhaps not the life we dreamed of when we were younger, but a good one all the same."

The Chinese girl tapped softly on the door and then entered carrying a silver tray with china cups, teapot and dessert plates. Miette and Hannah smiled to each other as they ate the berry pies. Together they spent the afternoon reminiscing about the decade that had passed since their stagecoach ride to Angels Camp.

That evening Hannah beamed her pleasure as she greeted customers arriving at *Maison de Paris* for dinner. With Miette's blessing, she took over the greeter's role at the front entrance, giving a special greeting, with warm embraces to the people who had answered Miette's summons to a special dinner party.

"Glory be, look at you. If you're not a sight for sore eyes."

"Hello, Emma. How do you like my dress?"

Emma Laughten stopped to stare. "Is that the gown I think it is?"

"Made by you and displayed in your shop window the first time I came to San Francisco. Remember how I admired it?"

"I do remember. Bright red with silver inset panels and embroidery. Oh, mercy, you were a sight the first time you tried it on. You're a lovely sight now, too. But styles have changed. That gown is long out of fashion. You need to have a crinoline or a hoop underneath that skirt now."

Hannah laughed. "You are right, of course. Time moves on and styles change. I have a large collection of gowns in France now, but I wanted you to see this wonderful dress the way it was when you sewed it. Will Sophie be along?"

"Indeed she will. Did you know she and Pádraig got married two years back? They'll be along as soon as they get the wee one to sleep. That dumb Irishman finally woke up to the fact Sophie was the best girl in the world for him. Now they have a sweet little lass. But Pádraig's talking about going east to fight if there's a war. God have mercy there isn't. And his good friend Diego Austen is a state senator, back and forth from Santa Barbara to Sacramento, so we see him often. He's married to a Californio girl, but no children yet"

Hannah fondly embrace Emma and pointed her up the stairs to the private room where the rest of her guests were gathering, telling her she'd be along as soon as all the guests arrived. Then she turned to the next person in line.

"Good evening," she said to a man with graying sandy-colored hair she didn't recognize. He was older, perhaps late forties or early fifties, but still had a youthful appearance. "I don't believe I know you."

"No reason you should, ma'am. Just got here from Boston. Arrived last week."

"Do you have a reservation then?"

"I don't. But I hear this is the finest restaurant in San Francisco."

"It is. We'll find you a table. What's your name, sir?"

"Thornton," the man said, "Will Thornton."

Hannah's heart dropped into her stomach. For a moment she was confused, the restaurant seemed to spin around her. Then she regained her composure and looked Will Thornton squarely in the eye. "I'm Hannah," she told him. "You might remember my mother."

HISTORICAL NOTE

WHEN CAPTAIN JOHN Charles Frémont led his band of California Volunteers over the Santa Ynez Mountains to the little village of Santa Barbara on Christmas Eve 1846, the Mexican War finally became a reality for the Californio men and women living there. Many of Frémont's men carried their saddles because none of the rancheros along his line of march would sell him new horses. He was forced to requisition them in Santa Barbara. Delfina de Alba Austen's Cañada del Corral, a small rancho on the coast, north of Rancho Dos Pueblos, was an obvious place to find quality horses and a good starting point for the story. After that, Frémont disappears from our narrative, marching further south to fight an inconsequential battle, but he continues to figure prominently in our story.

One of my pleasures in writing *Their Golden Dreams* was being able to juxtapose historic figures with my fictional characters in scenes that modeled real historic events. Imagining Delfina Austen standing up to John Frémont, or Pádraig Duggan debating slavery with Senator William Gwin, were exciting scenes for me to write. I have tried hard to ensure the integrity of the historic figures while giving readers a sense of the roles they played in California in the 1850s. Charles Grenough was not an historic figure so I was free to portray him as I chose. I alone am responsible for the fictional characters in the story that are wholly my creations and do not represent any real people.

In 1848, when the Mexican War ended, gold was discovered on the American River, and Frémont was in Washington, D.C. being court martialed for insubordination. He returned to California as the owner of Las Mariposas, one of the richest

Their Golden Dreams

gold strikes in the southern mines in 1849. As California strove for statehood in 1850, he was elected one of its first two senators, but drew only the two year term, and by the time California was admitted to the Union, and he was seated, he had little impact on legislation effecting the state. William Gwin, born in Tennessee and a Mississippi politician, got the six-year term and was far more influential in the affairs of the state.

In 1856, General Frémont preceded Abe Lincoln as the first candidate of the Republican Party for President of the United States. He lost, partially because of his free soil politics and partially because his wife, Jessie Benton Frémont, meddled in the campaign.

Ironically, the Treaty of Guadalupe Hidalgo ending the War was signed by the Mexican Government two weeks after John Marshall made his world-changing gold discovery at the lumber mill in Coloma. It was too late for Mexico, and the start of one of the largest voluntary migrations the world has ever seen. Later that year Lieutenant William Tecumseh (Billy) Sherman carried a sample of gold back to Washington to show President James K. Polk. Polk made the official announcement of the discovery to the startled nation in his December speech to Congress and the stampede to California was on. Long before that, Mormon apostate Sam Brannan had raced through the streets of San Francisco shouting, "Gold! Gold on the American River!"— the true start of the Gold Rush when San Francisco became an overnight ghost town. Brannan bought up all the picks, pans and shovels he could find and got far richer selling them than most of the miners who paid his exorbitant prices.

If the discovery of gold in 1848 was one of the major events of the year, it wasn't the only one. Revolutions wracked Europe. The one in France was especially devastating, and was followed by an economic depression. As a result large contingents of Frenchmen organized companies and set sail for the gold diggings in 1849. They represented a high percentage of the foreign miners in the southern mining district, second only to the Mexicans, Chileans, and, of course, Americans. (The mass immigration of Chinese came later.) Between 1849 and 1851 more than four thousand French flocked to California. The French Government raised money by selling lottery tickets; the winners got free passage to California. French women of easy virtue were plentiful in gold rush California, too. It was charged that the French Government used the lottery prizes to relocate prostitutes to California, and in at least one instance a French entrepreneur invested in the passage for about sixty of these women.

Hannah Runyon and Caroline Peabody came to California by ship, walking and riding mules across the Isthmus of Panama from an East Coast steamship to another steamer traveling up the West Coast. It was the fastest way to the gold fields, also the most expensive. Panama was then a part of the country of New Granada, which later became part of Columbia. Sailing around Cape Horn at the tip of South America was longer, but generally quicker than the least expensive overland route. The traffic across the Isthmus was far greater than the capacity of the steamships, forcing long layovers in Panama City, where rampant disease seemed to be a way of life.

With so many people, from so many nations, fighting for space on the Sierra's rivers and streams, and their share of the riches, conflict was inevitable. The Americans, new owners of California, tended to believe miners from other nations had no right to be in the foothills. A pie fight in Hannah's cafe is a metaphor for the continuous strife between the Yankees and those they thought guilty of stealing the state's wealth. There is no question many of the foreigners, primarily Mexicans, Chileans, and Chinese were mistreated. In the lawless mining camps in the foothills justice (as well as injustice) was swift. There is an abundance of first hand accounts in print about travel to the gold fields and the rough life there that make fascinating reading.

While clearly not foreigners, the Native American population suffered terribly at the hands of the Yankee newcomers. At Clear Lake, in what is now Lake County in 1850, the U.S. Army was called out to massacre an unarmed band of Pomo Indians. Their crime was the temerity to fight back against Andrew Kelsey and his partner who had all but enslaved them and committed murder and tortured them at slight provocation. Ben Kelsey stormed through Napa County looking for Indians to kill. (His wife, Nancy, is reputed to have been the woman who sewed the first Bear Flag during that ill-fated revolt.) The first governor of California, in a speech to the legislature, set the stage for the mistreatment of Indians by calling for their "extermination." On the other hand, the laws established by miners to govern themselves in the mining camps set precedents that found their way into California's legal codes.

Freezing to death while panning for gold dust and nuggets was far from the only path to riches in the Sierra foothills. Many a woman took in more gold by supplying miners with some memory of home, whether it was a clean tent, freshly washed clothing or warm, fresh baked berry pies.

San Francisco was the major beneficiary of the two billion dollars worth of gold that came out of the gold fields in the 1850s. Inflation was rampant, but if you had gold it didn't seem to matter. Eggs cost $3 each, the equivalent to $83 today; beef was $10 a pound, boots $6 and Sam Brannan's shovels cost $36, which would be over $1,000 in today's currency. San Francisco was a man's town with few diversions. Gambling was popular; prostitution ran a wide gambit from the pricy ladies at Pacific House (a product of fiction, but similar to historic accounts) to the singsong Chinese girls who were essentially sex slaves. As the decade of the 1850s wore on more women came to California to be with their husbands. Schools and churches were started and a more genteel element gradually replaced the rowdiness. The literature of the day always referred to San Francisco as "the City" with a capital C. I've retained that usage as a kind of homage to the period.

California's part in the build up to the Civil War is generally little known, but the state was a major player in the drama. California became the 31st state in the nation in 1850 without ever having been a territory in a rush precipitated by the Gold fever. The debate in the U.S. Congress was heated because California disrupted the balance of power between northern and southern states. The Civil War was delayed for a decade by the Compromise of 1850 that allowed California into the union, delayed but not canceled.

The compromise consisted of five separate bills passed by Congress. Virtually all of them were disliked by someone. Briefly, the bills passed that allowed California statehood were: 1.The slave trade was abolished in the District of Columbia; 2. The territory of Utah was organized with the principle of popular sovereignty, meaning its citizens would decide for themselves whether to be a free or slave state; 3. The territory of New Mexico was organized the same way; 4. Texas gave up its claim to its western lands in exchange for a $10 million reduction in its debt to the national treasury; 5. A much harsher Fugitive Slave Law was enacted. It required fugitive slaves captured in northern states to be returned to their southern masters by northerners.

Their Golden Dreams

With southern Democrat William Gwin serving the six-year term as senator, California became a Democratic Party-dominated state. It appears that Gwin's motive from the outset was to bring slavery to California. His first move was to lead Congress in the creation of a Land Commission that would review all Mexican Land Grants to determine their legality. This was in direct contradiction of the Treaty of Guadalupe Hidalgo ending the Mexican War, and began the process of breaking up large land holdings. The rancheros on those land grants were typically "land rich" but without enough money to pay for legal representation before the Land Commission that met only in San Francisco and conducted business only in English. Attorneys were frequently paid with land and those landowners who could not substantiate their claims lost everything. (Readers of my first novels, *Dream Helper* and *Delfina's Gold* will remember that Delfina never had a legal ownership of her beloved Cañada del Corral.)

The Democratic Party was bitterly divided during the decade of the 50s between Free-Soilers and Gwin's southern backers called the Chivalry or Chivs. Among the strategies considered to bring slavery to California was the concept of dividing the state in two, with southern California becoming a new, slave state. The conflict between the two wings of the Democratic Party became so hateful that state retired Attorney General David S. Terry, and U.S. Senator David C. Broderick—both Democrats and good friends—fought a duel at Lake Merced on September 13, 1859. Terry was pro-slavery and Broderick was abolitionist. Broderick died as a result of his wound.

As Civil War approached, the U.S. Army arrested some of the southern sympathizers, but most of the rest fled home to the south. There was no fighting in California during the war, and it remained in the Union, with only a small group of Californios joining the Union Army. But California's gold played a major role in the final outcome of the conflict.

Two quick notes:

First, gold was valued at $16 an ounce in San Francisco, approximately $450 today. About $1250 2019

And second, Stockton was not called Stockton when Diego and Hannah arrived there. It was called Tuleburg, but that seemed too confusing for readers so I kept the more recognizable name Stockton. Other names for it were Fat City and Mudville. Stockton was incorporated July 31, 1850.

If you have enjoyed reading this novel please post a positive review on Amazon, Goodreads and your other favorite book sites. Thank you for reading.

Other Novels by Willard Thompson
The Chronicles of California:
Dream Helper
Delfina's Gold
Their Golden Dreams

Also
The Girl from the Lighthouse

www.ingramcontent.com/pod-product-compliance
Lightning Source LLC
Chambersburg PA
CBHW020645300426
44112CB00007B/249